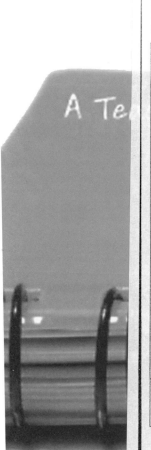
Study
skills

A Tutorial Programme for Students in Schools and Colleges

A Lucky Duck Book

Study
Skills

A Teaching Programme for Students in Schools and Colleges

Pat Guy

P·C·P

Paul Chapman
Publishing

First published 2007

Paul Chapman Publishing
A SAGE Publications Company
1 Oliver's Yard
55 City Road
London EC1Y 1SP

SAGE Publications Inc.
2455 Teller Road
Thousand Oaks, California 91320

SAGE Publications India Pvt Ltd
B 1/I 1 Mohan Cooperative Industrial Area
Mathura Road, New Delhi 110 044

SAGE Publications Asia-Pacific Pte Ltd
33 Pekin Street #02-01
Far East Square
Singapore 048763

Library of Congress Control Number: 2006931818

British Library Cataloguing in Publication data

A catalogue record for this book is available from British Library

ISBN-978-1-4129-2254-8
ISBN-978-1-4129-2255-5 (pbk)

Typeset by C&M Digitals (P) Ltd., Chennai, India
Printed on paper from sustainable resources
Printed in India at Replika Pvt. Ltd

Contents

Foreword

Go into any bookshop or type 'Study Skills' into your search engine and you will find a wealth of books and online resources which advise and instruct the conscientious student who is motivated to improve academic achievement. I can't help thinking that if the student can manage to read, understand, practise and change study habits as a result of this learning opportunity then he or she is already a pretty competent student.

From what I remember from my career relationships with underachieving students they usually need much more support than this. Firstly, and crucially, the step has to be taken to achieve an internal locus of control – that is, 'I am going to do this for myself and not because my teacher/parent/carer is pleading with or nagging me'. In this programme the author involves students from the start in assessing and understanding the blocks and obstacles, and in opportunities to self-manage their learning goals.

Secondly, when working in groups of young people with similar experiences of failure, non-comparative assessment techniques and enjoyable activities clearly related to the objectives will engage the student more actively in the task.

Thirdly, in her quest for continuing motivation from her students Pat Guy introduces some very interesting topics to help these young people to value and develop a range of talents associated with success, making this programme very different from the 'remedial' support that many of them will have previously experienced.

The final ingredient is for you, the tutor, to introduce and make significant. Reflect upon your own talents and weaknesses. Are you great at knitting, cooking, singing, dancing? As adults we are able to choose to enjoy our successes and avoid some of our failures, especially in public. I cannot knit so I buy my sweaters. I am not forced to struggle with needles and yarn, in front of my peers, and wear the resulting garment. That would damage my self-esteem, yet for many young people in school that is exactly what has happened to them. They have been forced to do more of what they are bad at and in public – no wonder they survive by avoidance or by disguising failure in disaffection.

> ... You've got to help me. You've got to hold out your hand even when that's the last thing I seem to want or need ... Each time you are kind and gentle and encouraging, each time you try to understand because you really care, my heart begins to grow wings, very small wings, very feeble wings, – but wings. (From *Glad to be Me*, edited by Don Peretz Elkins, 1976)

This is just the resource you need to help you to hold out your hand!

Barbara Maines

Lucky Duck

Introduction

Schools are currently experiencing a shift of focus away from students acquiring factual knowledge and towards metacognition or learning how to learn. Lessons in study skills make up one of the responses that schools have made to accommodate this new emphasis.

Lessons

These lessons have been designed for non-specialists wishing to cover an aspect of study skills during one-to-one lessons, small group tutorials, PHSE sessions, or in General Studies or subject lessons. The outlines are flexibly structured so that it is possible to select what is appropriate to an individual's or a group's needs. There is also an emphasis on pupil involvement in the lessons to ensure effective learning.

Although there is overlap in most topics, for ease of reference subjects have been organised under eight chapter headings. There will be areas in which cross-references can be made, so it may prove useful for the reader to skim through all of the chapters initially.

Pupil Advice Sheets, Activities and Questionnaires

Each chapter has self-help advice sheets for pupils. Are these resources can be printed from the CD-Rom and used during the lessons.

Resources

Although numerous targeted resources are available commercially, it is possible to use everyday materials in lessons to limit excessive financial outlay. Effective learning does not always require sophisticated equipment or expensive resources.

Pupils will require paper and writing equipment for recording in some lessons. Before starting the programme, provide each student with a ring file for questionnaires and worksheets. In the first session give pupils a plan of the topics that will be covered during the lessons and a copy of the glossary for reference.

Use the lessons as an opportunity to demonstrate good practice: ask the pupils to label their files clearly with their name, form and subject, to date each piece of work, to hole punch and file notes and worksheets immediately after each lesson, to use coloured sheets to divide the file into sections and to create their own lists of spellings, notes and definitions at the back.

1

A Study Skills Questionnaire

The purpose of the questionnaire is to highlight those areas of study skills in which pupils lack confidence. Most pupils will know which aspects of their work could be improved.

As students move through the key stages, pressure on their time increases. For teachers to put effective support strategies into place, the strategies must have a clearly defined purpose. If a blanket approach to teaching study skills is used, pupils may feel they are practising previously mastered techniques and motivation will decrease. If an individual has a problem remembering French vocabulary, is constantly reprimanded for indecipherable handwriting or has little idea of how to structure an essay, self-interest will motivate them to work on these skills.

- The questionnaire could be discussed orally during a lesson, with an individual or a small group of pupils, then pupil response used to target an appropriate input.

- If the questionnaire was completed in written form, it could be used as a way of setting a year group for a differentiated input during PHSE lessons, with pupil responses highlighting areas of need. This could, for example, take the form of one large group for revision techniques, two groups for reading speed and three small groups to work on either spelling, memory or attention.

- The questionnaire could equally be used as a general introductory activity to draw pupils' attention to the many skills that underpin learning.

Study Skills Questionnaire

Reading

1 Do you read for pleasure? What sort of reading material do you choose? Do you enjoy any specific authors?

2 When reading silently, do you read word for word?

Yes/No/Sometimes

3 Would you use different reading techniques in different situations, for example, when reading a newspaper, school text, a fiction book or a magazine?

Yes/No/Sometimes

4 Do you have enough time to complete reading tasks set in class or for homework?

Yes/No/Sometimes

Memory

1 What techniques do you use when revising for tests and exams? Examples might include: question and answer sessions with friends, highlighting texts, mnemonics, keeping summaries of information on file cards, creating mind maps or reading notes onto tape.

2 Can you remember French vocabulary and scientific and mathematical formulae easily?

Yes/No/Sometimes

3 Can you remember sequences easily, for example, the order of the stages required to solve a mathematical problem?

Yes/No/Sometimes

4 Do you know how *you* learn most effectively: through practical activities, watching a video, discussing information or by listening to talks and lectures?

Attention

1   Can you listen throughout a lesson or does your attention wander?

Yes/No/Sometimes

2   If you do have a problem with concentration, what do you do?

3   Do you always participate fully in lessons?

Yes/No/Sometimes

4   When you are asked a question or to repeat instructions, are
    you always able to remember what has been said?

Yes/No/Sometimes

Organisation

1   Do you regularly forget equipment, homework and sports kit?

Yes/No/Sometimes

2   Are your desk, bedroom, and school bag so untidy that you
    cannot find your equipment or possessions?

Yes/No/Sometimes

Note taking

1   Can you always pick out the important facts from information?

Yes/No/Sometimes

2   How do you take notes? Do you, for example, mind map, listen and then jot brief notes
    down later, write out a few key points or take down information in long-hand?

3   Can you make notes and listen at the same time?

Yes/No/Sometimes

Essays

1 Do you always understand what an essay title is asking you to do?

Yes/No/Sometimes

2 Do you find it difficult to get started with an essay?

Yes/No/Sometimes

3 Do you have a problem with planning essays? Do you know what to include and what to leave out?

Yes/No/Sometimes

4 Do you have a good grasp of basic grammar and punctuation?

Yes/No/Sometimes

5 Are you aware of the main strengths and weaknesses that teachers identify in your essays: for example, good ideas that need expanding, not answering the question set or too much irrelevant detail?

Spelling

1 Has spelling ever been a problem for you?

Yes/No/Sometimes

2 Does it take you a long time to look up words in a dictionary?

Yes/No/Sometimes

3 Do you use a hand held or computer spellchecker?

Yes/No/Sometimes

4 Can you proofread accurately?

Yes/No/Sometimes

Presentation of Work

1 Is your handwriting legible?

Yes/No/Sometimes

2 Are your diagrams and maps neat and easy to read?

Yes/No/Sometimes

3 Can you write quickly enough to complete tasks within the allotted time?

Yes/No/Sometimes

4 Are you often disappointed with the appearance of your work? Do you try to be neat, but is your work still untidy?

Yes/No/Sometimes

5 Do you hands ache if you write for more than ten or fifteen minutes?

Yes/No/Sometimes

Exams and Revision

1 Do you find revision difficult? Which aspect do you find most difficult: for example organisation of the work to be covered, understanding previous work, getting started or knowing what topics to revise?

```
┌─────────────────────────────────────────────────────────────────┐
│                                                                   │
│                                                                   │
│                                                                   │
│                                                                   │
└─────────────────────────────────────────────────────────────────┘
```

2 Are the grades you get for exams the same as grades you get for course work?

Yes/No/Sometimes

3 Do your exam results reflect the effort you make to revise?

Yes/No/Sometimes

4 Do you get unduly anxious about the exams themselves?

Yes/No/Sometimes

Group Work and Oral Presentations

1 Are you able to give confident oral presentations?

Yes/No/Sometimes

2 Can you work as a member of a group?

Yes/No/Sometimes

3 Do you enjoy group work?

Yes/No/Sometimes

2

Learning Styles and Multiple Intelligences

Learning Styles and their Relevance in Schools

Knowledge about **how** they learn will help pupils to maximise success.

It is important that pupils realise that they are in control of their study, and that it is in their interest to recognise and use those strategies that work best for them. Encouraging pupils to take responsibility for their own learning will prepare them for life beyond school.

Learning style questionnaires can help pupils identify their preferred ways of working. Subsequent lessons can build on this knowledge, giving strategies for working with strengths and supporting weaknesses.

Pupil responses to any questionnaire will be dependent upon their interpretation of each question and their mood at the time. Additional factors such as personality traits, educational experience and levels of maturity will influence their answers. Results cannot be seen as inflexible truths.

In an ideal world, differences in learning preferences would be compensated for by teaching staff differentiating all of their lessons to match each individual's needs. However, such perfection is hard to achieve and it is up to students to help themselves as much as possible.

Basic learning style questionnaires divide individuals into three broad groups: these consist of visual learners; kinaesthetic learners; auditory learners.

- Visual learners prefer a visual input to lessons and appreciate the use of diagrams and visual aids to support their learning. They work best when given an overview of the information. They will have a tendency to daydream and find it hard to listen for extended periods.

- Auditory learners will find listening easy and enjoy lectures and discussions. Such learners will have a good recall of any information that is presented orally.

- Kinaesthetic learners have a tendency to fidget, will enjoy physical activity and remember best by doing. They use gesture to explain themselves and work most effectively in short bursts.

The results of the questionnaires will show different pupils to have different balances of learning styles.

Some pupils will have one preferred learning style. They may learn efficiently in practical sessions, but lose concentration in lectures (a kinaesthetic preference); enjoy videos, but loath role-play (a visual preference); or love discussion but hate mind mapping (an auditory preference).

These groups of pupils will need support to work out strategies to help themselves learn more effectively in classroom situations that do not suit their style. The group that will have to make the most adaptations will be kinaesthetic learners. This is because traditionally teaching has tended to be carried out in an auditory style, the 'chalk and talk' approach with some additional visual input.

Those who have achieved at school in the past will have been individuals who have succeeded in a predominantly auditory learning environment; some will have continued into higher education and become teachers. If these individuals achieved success when taught in an auditory way, they will assume that this teaching style is the most effective, and so the same cycle is repeated. This will handicap those pupils who need to 'do' in order to understand.

Other pupils will have a balance of learning styles and will be able to adapt relatively easily to a variety of classroom situations: this group will be in the best position to take advantage of their school experience.

Lesson Plan

Learning objective

Pupils will have a greater understanding of their preferred learning styles, and be able to use this knowledge to help themselves to learn more effectively.

Resources required

- The Learning Style questionnaire.
- Highlighters or coloured pencils.
- A whiteboard or OHP (overhead projector).

Activities

The Learning Style questionnaire (see pages 12–13) could be distributed prior to the session for pupils to complete as homework, or alternatively could be completed as part of the session.

Individual learning styles can be recorded on the whiteboard or OHP. Each pupil writes down their visual, auditory and kinaesthetic scores in grid form on the board.

This will raise pupil (and staff) awareness of the range of learning styles that exist in every group, as it is easy to imagine that everyone learns in the same way as you.

The Pupil Advice Sheet (see pages 14–15) can be distributed and discussed in small groups.

Discussion pointers could be:

1. Which members of the group have a balance/imbalance of learning styles?

2. Do the learning style descriptors ring true? Do visual and kinaesthetic learners have more of a problem with attention in the classroom than the auditory learners?

3. If learners have problems in a lesson that is taught in only one style, how could they help themselves? What could teachers do to help?

4. List the lesson preferences for the pupils to see if there is any match between learning styles and the lessons pupils enjoy.

5. Can the pupils explain why they like some lessons more than others? Could this be a result of their learning preferences?

6. What learning strategies do pupils currently use?

7. Do they use different strategies in different subject lessons?

8. Are some of the strategies suggested ones that they have used in the past, but found incompatible to their way of working? Why was that?

At this stage each group highlights in one colour the ideas from the pupil advice sheet that are most popular within their group and those that are most unpopular in another colour.

To ensure all students participate, discussion of the questionnaire results can build into whole-class discussion through the 'snowball' technique. This involves each small group working together on their initial responses and then joining with a second group to share their findings before moving into a whole-class discussion.

A whole-class analysis of the most popular strategies from the pupil advice sheet can be recorded on the whiteboard, for example:

- Ten people summarise notes on to index cards when revising.
- Five people use background music to help them to concentrate.
- Twelve people highlight their notes to pick out key points.
- Four pupils use mind-mapping techniques.

Each pupil identifies some of the different methods described by the others to trial for themselves during the following week.

Finally one pupil presents a problem, for example:

- 'I can never remember scientific formulae'.
- 'I find it hard to learn Modern Foreign Language (MFL) vocabulary'.
- 'I can't concentrate in History; the teacher talks too much'.
- 'I don't understand Physics. It is just too boring'.

The rest of the class have to suggest possible solutions to the problems and say if these strategies would be appropriate for visual, auditory or kinaesthetic learners.

Learning Style Questionnaire

Give yourself a mark out of five for each statement:

5 = agree strongly

4 = this would be true for most of the time

3 = regularly happens

2 = occasionally true

1 = hardly ever happens

Section A

1   In activities that involve discussion or listening, do you lose concentration easily? ☐

2   Do you find instructions that are only given orally difficult to recall? ☐

3   When learning about something new, would you rather watch a video than listen to a visiting speaker? ☐

4   In a class discussion do you watch and think, rather than talk and interact? ☐

5   Do you find it difficult to remember jokes that you have been told? ☐

6   Would you rather be shown how to do something, than told how to? ☐

7   Do you doodle during lessons? ☐

8   Do you have difficulties generally with concentration? ☐

9   Is your handwriting clear and neat? ☐

10 Do you understand and memorise information more effectively if you are able to see it in diagram, map or graphic form? ☐

Total Points = ☐

Section B

1   Do you find it difficult to sit still, fidgeting and moving about more than your peers? ☐

2   Do you have a talent for making things? ☐

3   Do you use your hands to emphasise points and seem animated when talking? ☐

4   Do you dress for comfort, with a preference for casual over formal clothes? ☐

5   Are you weak at spelling? ☐

6　Do you prefer games with action and noise to quieter games like chess?　☐

7　Do you often refer to things as 'whatsits' or 'thingamajigs'?　☐

8　Are you outgoing and extrovert by nature?　☐

9　Do you like to solve problems by working them through in a practical way?　☐

10　Do you feel irritated if you have to sit and listen for long periods?　☐

Total Points = ☐

Section C

1　Do you enjoy talking and discussion?　☐

2　Do you find it easy to remember oral instructions?　☐

3　Do you prefer to listen to music rather than look at art or design?　☐

4　Are you easily distracted by noise and prefer a quiet environment for working?　☐

5　Do you enjoy crosswords and other word puzzles?　☐

6　Do you enjoy group work?　☐

7　Do you remember things that you have heard rather than things that you have seen?　☐

8　Do you like to listen to the radio?　☐

9　Do you enjoy riddles and puns?　☐

10　Do you hum and sing to yourself more than your peers?　☐

Total Points = ☐

Write down your total score for Section A. TOTAL SCORE = —— / 50

This score will relate to your visual learning preference.

Write down your total score for Section B. TOTAL SCORE = —— / 50

This score will relate to your kinaesthetic learning preference.

Write down your total score for Section C. TOTAL SCORE = —— / 50

This score will relate to your auditory learning preference.

Pupil Advice Sheet (Learning Styles)

Everyone learns in different ways. You may have preferences in the way you work that are linked to your learning style. Look below at the advice for learning listed for your particular preference: see if you already use some of the methods or if these might be ways you could learn in the future.

If you are a Kinaesthetic Learner

Some pupils will favour a kinaesthetic learning style. These individuals will learn best when they are involved in learning (i.e. 37% of learners have a kinaesthetic learning preference).

- Work from whole to part. When you read a textbook, look at the pictures, diagrams, summaries and chapter headings. Read any conclusions first, and then work back to the beginning: this will help you to understand how the sections of information fit together.

- If you need to fidget in class, cross your legs and bounce the foot that is off the floor so that you don't disturb others.

- When working at home, play familiar music in the background to screen out distractions.

- Walk around as you read information out. Chant verb endings as you walk up and down the stairs.

- Use coloured transparencies over texts when reading to cut the glare of black print on white paper and add novelty to hold your attention.

- Use coloured paper as a desk blotter behind reading material. This will help you to focus on the text.

- Think of practical applications or everyday examples of theoretical knowledge to help with understanding. Thinking along these lines is not a waste of time: engaging your brain will make information more memorable.

- When working at home, if you find it difficult to study at a desk, lie on your bed or on the floor.

- When working, take regular breaks and allow yourself to move about. It will be easier for you to concentrate if you study for short periods and then stop for a while. Work for 30 minutes, then go and get a drink/clean your shoes/wash your hair/put a few CDs back in their cases – then start working again.

If you are a Visual Learner

Twenty nine per cent of the population are visual learners. They will learn best when they can see and visualise information.

- Write information down, then summarise, copy out and rewrite it in a variety of handwriting styles.

- Most visual learners learn best when working independently in a quiet place. Some individuals find that playing background music can aid concentration, particularly when doing Maths.

- Use coloured pens, coloured paper and highlighters to make notes visually appealing.

- Translate information into mind maps, diagrams and charts to make you think about and restructure facts. This will allow you to become more aware of any links between information.

- Highlight your own books or any photocopies from school textbooks.

- You may find videos, perhaps of set texts, useful to give you background information and stimulate your curiosity about a topic.

- Try to sit away from visual distractions in the classroom: windows, doors, and amusing peers.

- Use computers to support your learning: educational games, encyclopaedic or revision CDs.

If you are an Auditory Learner

Thirty four per cent of the population are auditory learners. They will learn best when they listen to information.

- Work with others. Discussion and argument will help you to organise your ideas and remember facts.

- Summarise work (revision notes, MFL vocabulary and quotes) on to tapes and listen to the information while in the bath/walking the dog/travelling in the car, and before going to sleep.

- Teach someone else. This works particularly well if the person is unfamiliar with the information and you have to be very precise and clear in your explanations.

- Use mnemonics, rhythm and music to aid memory.

- Use tapes of, for example, set texts or language tapes, to support and extend your learning.

- Read texts and notes aloud in different voices and with different accents.

- When working alone, it will be easier to work in a quiet place away from distractions.

- Write questions and answers on cards and ask friends or family to test you.

Multiple Intelligences

The following lesson plan is useful to enhance pupils' self-esteem.

Howard Gardner (1993) argues that there are more forms of intelligence than are acknowledged in school, where there is an emphasis on linguistic skills and logical-mathematical ability. This can mean that the ability of individuals showing talent in areas such as music, design, sport, drama, ICT, leadership or art, may go unrecognised.

It is useful for pupils to appreciate that a variety of skills is necessary to get on in life. Being thought of as intelligent at school does not necessarily equate to success in the workplace, where social skills, hard work and motivation may be more highly valued.

Pupils who do not achieve highly at school are often those who have the life skills necessary to achieve in the real world. The fact that pupils have experienced a degree of frustration or disappointment at school will have taught them valuable lessons about perseverance and empathy.

> I had to train myself to focus my attention. I became very visual and learnt how to create mental images in order to comprehend what I read. (Tom Cruise – actor)

> At the age of eight I still couldn't read, I was soon being beaten twice a week for doing poor class work or confusing the date of the Battle of Hastings. (Richard Branson – entrepreneur)

> I preferred art and geology because messing about with paint and rocks was fun. I like things to be touchy-feely. (Jamie Oliver – TV chef)

Lesson Plan

Learning objective
Students will realise that a variety of talents is necessary to be successful in life.

Resources required
- Pictures or photographs of famous personalities: sports people, musicians, film/television stars, politicians and entrepreneurs.
- A whiteboard or OHP.

Activities
Begin with class discussion. The teacher lists Gardner's seven intelligences (see Appendices, Howard Gardener's Multiple Intelligences) on the whiteboard and briefly explains the background to this theory and what each form of intelligence entails.

Pupils can suggest well-known individuals that exemplify the different intelligences.

Initially Gardner identified seven aspects of intelligence:

- Kinaesthetic   A wide range of practical aptitudes, dance, drama and creative skills. This intelligence will cover physical and sporting ability.

- Musical   Skill in composing and playing music and an appreciation of rhythm.

- Visual-Spatial   Artistic talent and visualisation skills. This intelligence is linked closely to practical creativity.

- Logical/mathematical   Ability with numbers and scientific thought. An individual with talent in this area will enjoy problem solving, precision, abstract thought and logic.

- Interpersonal   The ability to empathise and work with others. Individuals with this intelligence will be popular and enjoy social interaction.

- Linguistic   A skill in all forms of written and oral literacy: a general ability with language. Anyone with this intelligence will be gifted in reading, writing, listening and discussion.

- Intrapersonal   Good self-knowledge and understanding. Individuals with this form of intelligence will know how to motivate themselves and make the best of their abilities.

Distribute or display lists and photos of famous people: politicians, entrepreneurs, sportsmen and women, designers, inventors, engineers, musicians, scientists, artists and film stars. Have group or paired discussion about the different kinds of intelligences that these individuals will need. The groups can compare results as a class.

Then present each group with a list of occupations. What intelligences are necessary for: a parent, film producer, receptionist, farmer, musician, hairdresser, teacher, chef, architect, fashion buyer, taxi driver, doctor, accountant, priest, tennis player or a member of the police force? The pupils list three intelligences necessary for each job and why they chose these skills.

Working in pairs the students can identify the different intelligences that they each possess.

Gardner added a naturalist intelligence to his original seven intelligences for individuals, with an interest in the natural world. Could the groups suggest additional forms of intelligence? See Multiple Intelligences sheet in the appendices.

3

Reading

Reading Techniques

It may have been apparent from pupils' responses to the Study Skills Questionnaire that they do not read regularly enough to raise their reading levels. One way to improve an individual's reading is to ensure that they are aware of the different reading techniques they can use.

It is necessary to use different reading techniques when tackling different types of material. If a pupil is using the same technique to get an idea of the overall content of a book, to read an exam question or find a specific piece of information in an encyclopaedia, their reading is inefficient.

Lesson Plan

Learning objective
Pupils will be able to differentiate between different reading techniques and identify appropriate occasions for different techniques to be used.

Resources required
- A selection of holiday brochures, magazines, timetables, newspapers and directories.

Activities
The teacher explains and models skimming, scanning and close reading techniques.

- *To skim* is to glance through a text quickly to get the gist. Skimming would involve reading through the introductory paragraphs, any highlighted sections, headings and summaries, and looking at illustrations. A teacher could demonstrate this by modelling how to skim a chapter from a class text.

- *To scan* is to search a piece of text looking for something specific, perhaps a date, a place or a name. The subject teacher could model scanning by demonstrating how ineffective it would be to read a whole chapter from the class text to find one specific detail, but would show how to use an index, chapter headings and titles to target the search.

- *To read closely* is to read word for word. This is necessary when reading important information, for example, an exam question. Every word should be read and carefully considered.

Discuss whether it would be sensible to skim, scan or read closely in a variety of situations such as

- Looking for a phone number in the directory.

- Reading a mobile phone contract.

- Reading a long and boring letter from your aunt.

- Seeing if a programme is on television this evening.

- Looking at a gardening book to see if it would make a suitable present for your granddad.

- Looking for an item in a shopping list.

- Reading self-assembly furniture instructions.

- Looking at a library book to see if it will be useful for a project.

(See Reading Techniques in the Appendices)

Pupils now think of ten further examples where skimming, scanning or close reading would be appropriate techniques.

Use the extracts taken from newspapers and magazines as practice for skimming. Ask the pupils to write text messages summarising the gist of newspaper reports and articles from magazines.

Utilise recipes, timetables, holiday brochures, telephone directories and television programmes as suitable material for scanning. Ask pupils to work in pairs. Time them as they look up a set number of addresses in the phone book/times of ten television programmes/quotes from a class textbook/or the prices of six holidays.

Reading Speed

Slow, careful reading is essential when reading complex pieces of text. However, some pupils will read silently at the same pace at which they read aloud; this will put them at a disadvantage as they move through secondary school and are expected to read a greater volume of material. Lack of speed will deter them from reading for pleasure.

Practice does make perfect. It is possible to increase reading speed with regular practice.

As a result of the concentration necessary when reading for speed, the pupils' comprehension and recall will increase.

Lesson Plan

Learning objective
Pupils will understand how to increase their reading speed.

Resources required
- A class reader or suitable fiction text.

- Rulers.

- Stopwatches.

- A selection of different coloured A4 plastic overlays. (See Reading Techniques in the Appendices).

Activities

Measure reading speed

- Use a class reader to test pupils' present reading speed when reading aloud and when reading silently. Reading speed can be measured by pupils reading aloud for a minute and then calculating the average number of words they have read. Ask the pupils to count the number of words in four lines of text and divide the total by four to get an average number of words per line. Then multiply the average number of words per line by number of lines read to get a rate of words per minute. Repeat the process for silent reading. If the scores for reading aloud and reading silently are the same, then the pupil is reading word for word when reading silently and will be at a disadvantage. (See Increasing Silent Reading Speed in the Appendices)

- Ask each pupil to time their silent reading speed in this way each day for a week and to keep a daily record to see how much they improve with effort and practice.

- It is easier to use fiction texts initially: the vocabulary will be easier and poor comprehension of the text will not detract from the overall aim of increasing speed.

Model strategies that will increase reading speed

- Show the pupils how to look for key words to get the overall sense of the passage.

- Demonstrate how to use headings and summaries to eliminate sections that need not be read.

- Explain that there is no need to read every word. Pupils should take in chunks of words and try to read blocks of three or four words at a time.

- Explain that it is necessary to keep eyes moving steadily from left to right across the page and to avoid going back over text. The brain will become used to filling in any gaps.

- Demonstrate the use of a ruler as a tracking tool. Keep the ruler below the line being read and move the ruler down the page steadily, so that the eyes are forced to keep pace. Alternatively, pupils could track the text with a pen or finger to maintain speed.

- Experiment with coloured overlays. These can be made quite simply by cutting A4 coloured pockets in half. The use of these sheets as overlays will help some pupils by cutting down the distracting contrast between page and print.

- When reading for speed, concentration is vital: the pupil must be focused. Warn pupils that their concentration will drop when they are hungry, tired or uncomfortable.

- It is always worth checking that the light is adequate before starting to read. The eyes tire quickly when they are strained.

- Any limitations in vocabulary will slow down reading speed. Pupils should try to familiarise themselves with the meanings of any unknown words prior to reading. It may be worth the pupils targeting specific subjects; for example, if they find Geography texts hard to read at speed they should work on Geography vocabulary.

Pupil Advice Sheet (Reading Techniques)

Try to use different types of reading in different situations. It would be a waste of time to read all of a railway timetable just to see what time your train is leaving, or all of a sports page to see if your team had won their match.

- We skim read to get an overview of a text. You would skim the section on Christianity in an encyclopaedia to see if the information is relevant for your project.

- We scan a text to look for specific information: for example, a grandparent's grocery list to see if they need to buy coffee, or a calendar to confirm the date of a dental appointment.

- We need to read closely to check information thoroughly. A new mobile phone contract, or a question in an exam paper, must be read carefully to ensure understanding.

Reading speed

After moving into secondary school it becomes increasingly useful to be able to read quickly. This is a skill that can be developed with practice. Reading quickly will be harder with some materials than with others because of the words that are used. Novels will be easier than text on a complex subject.

To increase your reading speed, first choose a text that you can read comfortably with good understanding. Start at the beginning of a chapter and read for a minute. Count the number of words on any four separate lines that you have read and divide the total number by four to get an average number of words per line. Multiply this number by the total number of lines that you can read in one minute. This will give you your reading rate per minute. Record this score and use it as your baseline.

The following evening read another passage for a minute from the same book and record your reading rate again. Concentrate on reading as quickly as you can, but still try to absorb the meaning of the text. If you do this every evening for two weeks, you will find that your reading speed will gradually increase.

- Try to take in three or four words at a time rather than reading word for word.

- Do not allow yourself to backtrack to check on words but keep your eyes moving forwards. Your brain will fill in the gaps.

- Put a ruler or index card under the line that you are reading and move it steadily down the page to maintain pace. Alternatively, use your finger or pen as a pointer and move it along the line of print.

You can then begin to practise on more complex texts.

Some people find that a coloured plastic A4 sheet placed over the text reduces glare from the paper and makes reading more comfortable. Old A4 coloured file pockets can be cut in half and used for this.

If you get headaches when reading at length, it may be worth having your eyes checked by an optician.

4

Comprehension

Reading Comprehension

It is possible for all pupils to improve their understanding of a text or verbal information. Competent readers automatically use strategies to monitor comprehension as they read; other pupils will need to be taught how to do this.

Lesson Plan

Learning objective

Pupils will be able to approach a variety of reading tasks using techniques to support comprehension.

Resources required

- Photocopied articles from a magazine or newspaper as appropriate to the age of the pupils.

- Highlighters or coloured pencils.

Activities
A 'reading for understanding' approach

The teacher demonstrates the approach by reading a photocopied passage from a subject text or newspaper article. As the teacher talks through what she is doing and why, the pupils follow using their own photocopy.

- 'I read the title or heading to get an idea of the topic and how it fits into the present module'.

- 'Then I read the first few sentences to get an idea of what the passage will be covering. I highlight in one colour any key words that relate to this idea'.

- 'Then I read the rest of the passage to find the supporting evidence, which I highlight in another colour'.

- 'After reading, I summarise the main ideas for myself'.

- 'Then I jot down the gist of the passage in my own words'.

The pupils prepare a second summary in the same way with an alternative piece of text. This can be completed individually, as pairs or in a small group. Simple or complex text can be used as is appropriate to the individual or group.

SQ3R (Survey, Question, Read, Recall, Review)

McLean and Wood (2004) describe SQ3R as one method that can be used to read books in a purposeful way. The method enables pupils to make sense of and organise information. Their teacher once again models the technique, and the pupils practise the process individually or in pairs.

- Survey Look at the title and glance through the contents page and chapter headings to make sure that the book contains the information needed.

- Question   Why am I reading this? What do I need to find out? Which part is going to be most useful?

- Read   Read a targeted chapter, thinking about key words and looking closely at any illustrations, graphs and diagrams.

- Recall   Think about the chapter and what has been learnt, note down key facts, relate the information to prior knowledge and work out an example from everyday life.

- Review   Check that appropriate information has been taken from the book, recorded appropriately and understood.

Change written text into a diagram

This could be information taken from a class text, magazine or newspaper. The process of thinking about the information and how to convert it into a diagram will ensure pupils interact with the facts, thereby increasing their understanding. Examples might include:

- Plotting the career progress of a famous sporting or historical figure on a time line with illustrations.

- Converting the development of a geographical feature into diagramatic form.

- Illustrating the relationship between characters in a play or set book in the form of a mind map.

Pupil Advice Sheet (Comprehension)

- Use easier textbooks to help understanding. Year 6 texts rather than Year 7; Year 8 texts rather than Year 9. These books will help to sort out any confusion. The basic information will be similar but will be presented in a simpler way.

- Look closely at any diagrams in books. Diagrams will often show how facts link together in ways that you might not have realised.

- When reading from a passage, try to summarise the facts in your own words. Write out brief notes as if you were texting a friend.

- Enlarge complex, detailed text on a photocopier so that you can look at one section at a time.

- Ask other pupils to explain information. They may be able to explain a difficult concept in everyday language. People of your own age that have just grasped the concept themselves are more likely to understand your confusions than teachers, who have been familiar with the topic for years.

- Talk aloud to yourself. 'So what this is really saying is that …'. If you cannot summarise information in your own words, you have not understood it properly.

- Think about what you already know about the topic and how this new information fits with that.

- Pretend that you are teaching someone else the information.

- Draw a cartoon sequence of the events in a passage.

- Skim read a chapter before reading in depth to give you an idea of the content.

- Read difficult passages aloud. Reading a passage on to tape and then listening to it played back will leave you free to concentrate on the content.

- Summarise a passage in a mind map. Ensure that you record all of the key points.

- Highlight and then list all the facts, dates or names in a passage.

- Watching videos and television programmes or reading fiction related to a subject will add to your background knowledge and help with your understanding.

- If you are having problems reading *and* understanding a set book, borrow a taped version from the library. You can concentrate on understanding the storyline whilst someone else reads.

- Set English Readers are popular in the form of English as an Additional Language (EAL) texts. Libraries and bookshops will stock these series. The texts are simplified versions of the books and will give you an overview of the plot and characters. Some of the texts also have tapes that can be used alongside the books.

- Some schools will have differentiated textbooks. Read through the easiest ones.

- Run through recent work in your head before a lesson to refresh your memory.

- Ask a teacher to help with complex topics by explaining them in a different way, perhaps by drawing a diagram or relating the information to practical examples.

- Keep a dictionary or thesaurus handy to look up the meanings of unfamiliar words.

- Ask yourself the meanings of five words from the index of your class textbook each evening. The more subject words you understand, the better your comprehension will be.

Subject Specific Vocabulary

It is vital for pupils to have an understanding of subject specific words and their meanings if they are to improve their understanding of subject texts. Teaching staff can over estimate pupils' knowledge and assume understanding where none exists.

Many subject specific words have everyday equivalents that confuse students, for example, scientific words such as conductor, force, contract, positive, charge, cell, pupil, bulb and material. Just a few unfamiliar words within a text can limit pupil understanding.

Most subject departments will have systems giving pupils access to vocabulary lists. These might include:

- Subject specific vocabulary and definitions accessed through departmental web pages.

- Lists of words specific to a module distributed and discussed during the first lesson of the module.

- Vocabulary lists given to pupils at the beginning of each school year.

- Key word display boards kept with items of equipment and displayed in graphic form against the correct spelling and definition.

However, having vocabulary lists available does not guarantee that pupils will use them. Regular, short revision sessions in class will familiarise all of the pupils with the words and their correct definitions. Such ten minute long, quick-fire sessions can be used for a break within a lesson.

Lesson Plan

Learning objective
Pupils will be able to use and define subject specific vocabulary with confidence and accuracy.

Resources required
- Class textbooks.

- Post-it notes.

- Pre-prepared DARTS (Directed Activity Related to Text) procedures.

- A whiteboard or OHP.

- Small, blank cards for use in games.

Activities
The teacher selects from the following as appropriate.

- Use the word lists from the back of class textbooks. The pupils work in pairs. One pupil reads out the meaning of a word and then defines it in their own words clearly enough to satisfy their partner.

- 'What am I?' Write a word on a Post-it note. One pupil puts the note on their forehead or their back without looking at it. They have to ask the other pupils questions that require a yes or no response in order to work out who or what they are: rhombus, Lysander, monitor, photosynthesis, government, Mediterranean, Queen Victoria or an equilateral triangle. Working in pairs or small groups will ensure that everyone participates.

- Use Directed Activity Related to Text (DARTs) activities. DART activities would include: cloze procedures, completion of a partially drawn table, cutting and pasting definitions to the correct vocabulary or part of a diagram, and converting information into a diagram.

- Mnemonics can help draw pupils' attention to the meanings and correct spelling of subject vocabulary. For example, in equal, equilibrium, equation and equilateral, the root word is *equa/equi* from the Latin, 'to make even'. Homework activities could involve devising and illustrating a mnemonic to help remember the meaning of these words.

- 'Odd Man Out'. The teacher lists a group of words on the OHP or whiteboard. The pupils work out which word is the odd one out and why.

- Draw the pupils' attention to key word displays by having quizzes on the words and their definitions for five minutes at the beginning or end of a lesson.

- The equivalent of the board games 'Taboo' or 'Articulate' can be played where a specific word has to be described without using the word.

- Play 'Word Loops'. Each pupil in the class is given a few cards with a subject word on one half of the card and the definition of another word on the other half. One pupil starts by reading out the definition of a word that is on their card; the pupil with the corresponding word reads it out and then gives the definition that is on the other half of their card and so on. If the loop is run through a few times and timed, pupils will be motivated to respond as quickly as possible. The cards could be redistributed to different pupils at the end of each game to ensure attention.

- 'Bingo'. The pupils work in small groups and chose six words from the vocabulary list for that module. One pupil reads out definitions for the words from the list in a random order and the others cross off the corresponding word if it is on their grid. The first pupil with all of their words crossed off wins the game.

- 'Hangman' or 'Blockbusters' can be played in pairs, groups or as a whole-class activity. A pupil or the teacher can lead the game.

- Card games such as 'Pelmanism' can be played in pairs or small groups. If the pupils are involved in designing the cards or game, they will have discussed the words and their definitions before playing, giving an additional opportunity for revision.

- 'I went to market and bought ... '. A collection of objects or pictures of objects could be displayed on the OHP and removed when they are correctly named and a definition of their use given. For younger pupils in MFL or Science, objects could be laid out on a table.

General Vocabulary

Vocabulary plays a major part in reading and comprehension throughout life. A young child who is beginning to read would sound a word out letter by letter: c-a-t. If the child is unfamiliar with the meaning of the word 'cat' she would not understand what she had read and comprehension of the text would remain unclear. It is easy to imagine that a pupil can understand a text just because they are able to decode the words. Some pupils direct all of their energy into working out the pronunciation of words and have little idea of the meaning of a passage. This is common amongst weak readers: when reading in front of their peers, all of their effort will be focused on decoding the words and not on understanding the passage.

As pupils move through school it is possible for them to appear articulate, but at the same time only to be using conversational language and to have little comprehension of the formal language of texts. This will put them at a disadvantage in secondary school and further education.

For many students the most effective way to increase their receptive vocabulary is through reading. The more a pupil reads, the more extensive their vocabulary will be. The pupil that reads widely is at a distinct advantage in school. This is particularly the case with academic texts. A pupil can skip words and still have overall understanding of a fiction text, but this is impossible with subject texts.

Lesson Plan

Learning objective
The pupils will appreciate the importance of developing and extending their vocabulary.

Resources required
- Extracts from KS1, KS4 and/or A Level texts.
- A whiteboard or OHP.
- Thesauruses and dictionaries.

Activities
Introduce the topic
Point out that it is vital for individuals to continue to develop their vocabulary throughout life. By way of a demonstration, ask one pupil to read an extract from a Key Stage 1 reading book and a second (more confident reader) to read aloud from an A Level or postgraduate text. It will be obvious that pupils have made great developmental strides already, but that this development needs to continue.

Write a list of words on the board
Choose some words that pupils will use in conversation and others that are more obscure or likely only to appear in written texts. Ask the pupils to identify:

- those words they would use;
- those words they understand, but would not use;
- those words they have not met.

A list that might be appropriate for Key Stage 3 might be: sport, classrooms, duration, epicure, crosswords, blithe, bulwark, podium, shouting, tenuous, short, rescind and important. This will show that it is always possible to continue to learn new words and extend one's vocabulary. When working on vocabulary, it is most useful to focus on the words that a pupil recognises, but does not feel confident enough to use in oral or written work.

Use the following sessions

These work best as regular, short, fun inputs. Allow the pupils to work in pairs or small groups and choose from the activities as appropriate to pupil age and ability.

- How many compound words can pupils list in two minutes: tailgate, birdcage, haircut, eggcup, and netball? How many new compound words can be created in two minutes? (See Compound Words in the Appendices)

- Have pupils write a short passage that includes a few specific words: ousted, feeble, lethargy, isolated and perplexed. 'The lethargy of the old, feeble wolf isolated him from his perplexed family, and they ousted him from the pack'. (See Make up a Sentence that Uses Each Word in the Appendices)

- Have pupils design a quiz for one letter of the alphabet to test their peers. The clue must be a synonym. 'To supply = p—', 'To creep = p—', 'Strange = p—'. (See Dictionary Work in the Appendices)

- Pupils are to find the male equivalent of female words: nephew and niece; stallion and mare; maternal and paternal.

- Give pupils a list of sentences where one word is used repeatedly. Replace the word with more descriptive words. 'Walk' could be changed to 'stumbled', 'ambled', 'strolled', 'marched', 'hobbled' or 'sauntered'. (See Boring Words in the Appendices)

- Pupils grade objects according to size. Mansion, hovel, cottage, bungalow. Hamlet, town, village, city. Cherry, apple, mango, kiwi, melon. A million, a hundred, a thousand, ten. (See Hot and Cold in the Appendices)

- Pupils collect group terms: a swarm of bees, a litter of puppies, a bouquet of flowers, a pride of lions, a troupe of dancers.

- Pupils guess the definitions of unknown or nonsense words from a passage using context and grammatical knowledge. (See Using Context to Guess A Word in the Appendices)

- Set quizzes to be completed in two minutes. List as many types of dog, tree, colour, minerals, insects, sport, flower, and occupations as you can. List as many words related to: the coast, volcanoes, magnetism or electricity as you can.

Take the opportunity to use technical English vocabulary in context

- Discuss how to work out the meanings of words using prefixes and suffixes. For example: em = from; im = into; – ant = one who. Collections of words can be written on the board and their meanings deduced by pupils using prior knowledge and knowledge of the parts of words: emigrate, emigration, immigrant, migrant, immigrate and migratory.

- Look closely at synonyms and antonyms. Ask the pupils to write out their own lists of synonyms and put a decoy word in the list. Their partner then has to spot the odd one out: for example, definite, certain, indisputable, doubtful, sure.

- Make adjectives from nouns and nouns from adjectives: distant/distance; silk/silky; wise/wisdom.

- Write out sentences to show the different meanings and spellings of verbs and nouns: advice and advise; practice and practise; licence and license. Then illustrate the sentences to make a visually appealing mnemonic.

Dictionary Skills

Dictionaries and thesauruses are useful aids for extending vocabulary. Pupils need to use dictionaries and thesauruses regularly if they are to become familiar with their layout and purpose. Some pupils will need to be shown how to use the highlighted words at the top and bottom of the pages or the quartiles of a dictionary (A to E being the first quartile, E to M second, M to S third, and S to Z the fourth) to help locate a word.

When pupils are using a thesaurus, it is essential to discuss shades of meaning so that vocabulary is not used randomly. If pupils attempt to replace the words 'nice', 'good' and 'get' in a selection of sentences with more suitable words, it will become obvious that subtle differences of meaning exist between apparently similar words. The word 'nice' in 'a nice girl' and 'a nice picnic spot' cannot be replaced with the word 'friendly' in both cases.

Lesson Plan

Learning objective
Pupils become aware of the variety of strategies they can use to identify unfamiliar words.

Resources required
- Dictionaries and thesauruses.
- Photocopies of extracts from 'Old English' texts.

Activities
Play games with dictionaries and thesauruses as appropriate to pupils' ages and levels of understanding.

- Have question and answer sessions using the dictionaries. Pupils can make up quizzes for the rest of the class. Why would a farmer leave a field fallow? What part of a dog is its muzzle? What does an optometrist do? If we lament, are we sad or happy?

- Play 'Connections': start with a word from the dictionary. Each pair or group has to guess another word that will appear in the dictionary as a definition for that word. For example, the word 'seek' will appear as an alternative to the word 'search'. Pupils then guess a word that will appear as an alternative to 'seek'. The winners are the group able to make the longest unbroken chain of different words.

- Time the pupils as they look up a specified number of words. Record their individual times to show them how their competence will improve with practice.

- Look up the meanings of easily confusable words and clarify their definitions with cartoons, drawings or mnemonics: currant and current; adverse and averse; illegible and ineligible; empathic and empathise.

- Play 'Call my Bluff' in teams of three: find a word in the dictionary that will be unfamiliar to other pupils and record the word's definition. Make up two incorrect definitions for the word and present the three definitions to the rest of the class. The class have to guess which of the three definitions is correct.

- Pupils work in small groups and act out the meanings of words without using the actual word: hope, despair, fear, incredulity, despondency.

- Research the origins of words. *Specta* is Latin for 'to look' and therefore is part of our words: spectator, respectable, spectacles, inspect, prospect.

- Examine well known 'Old English' texts: such as *Pilgrim's Progress*, Shakespeare's plays or *The Canterbury Tales*, for modern-day vocabulary and words that reflected fashionable society of the time.

Visualisation as an Aid to Comprehension

One of the many benefits of reading aloud to children is that it gives them the opportunity to develop visualisation skills, that is, the ability to create the imaginary pictorial sequence of a story. For pupils who have only experienced storytelling on television or video visualisation may be an unfamiliar skill, but one that will have many benefits.

Visualisation is a useful technique to assist with understanding and memory. Many pupils will naturally visualise a sequence of information if they are given work that lends itself to that approach: a fictional passage, a parable or an historical event. However, not every pupil will be able to do this all of the time and in every situation.

Pupils may need encouragement initially to make their images multi-sensory; hearing the characters speak, smelling the dinner cooking, feeling the wooden bench that they are sitting on. Richly descriptive texts are most effective in early lessons as these give the most opportunity to develop this multi-sensory approach.

Younger pupils may need to scaffold images with drawings or a sequence of pictures initially.

Lesson Plan

Learning objective
Pupils will be able to visualise orally presented information and use the technique as a comprehension and memory tool.

Resources required
- Class reader or subject text.

Activities
- Ask the pupils to visualise their journey to school and draw simple representative pictures to illustrate the route: their house, the bus at the bus stop, the bus at the end of the street and then walking in through the school gates.

- Read a short passage from a class text. This could be the class reader or a non-fiction passage. The pupils close their eyes and make a video of the passage in their heads. They illustrate their video in simple cartoon form to represent the sequence of events.

- Read a longer passage or a passage with more detail. Ask the pupils to work in pairs and describe to their partner how they imagined the characters, objects or environment. Ask a variety of specific questions about the text to focus their attention on the detail. What did they imagine the main character was wearing? Were there any clues in the story to help or did they have to use their imagination? What prior knowledge did they use; for example, if the description were of a boy in the 1940s, would he be wearing trainers and a baseball cap? What season was being described and why did they think this? What did the friends look like?

- As the pupils become more experienced in the use of this technique, text and questioning can both become more complex and detailed.

5
Memory

Memory: How to make the most of it

The aim of any aspect of study skills lessons must be to increase pupils' knowledge about how they learn (metacognition) in order for them to learn to help themselves.

It is essential that pupils realise they must be listening and paying attention in order to remember information. Listening and concentration are essential parts of memorising.

Pupils' memories can be trained to retain more academic information as they progress through school. All pupils will benefit from being shown how the memory works and how to develop such skills.

The brain will instinctively try to order and sort information: it will judge what is worth remembering and discard the unimportant. The fact that a pupil can remember a friend's mobile phone number, but not a scientific equation, is a demonstration of their skill at prioritising information and the brain's effectiveness.

Always emphasise that it is easier to try to understand information than to try to remember facts by rote. Encourage pupils to link new information to existing knowledge and to think of practical, concrete examples of theoretical concepts (for example, boiling steam in a kettle producing water when it contacts a cold surface or magnetic catches on fridge doors). Pupils should ask for additional or alternative explanations of anything they have not understood.

Lesson Plan

Learning objective
Pupils are able to identify and to use a variety of memory techniques.

Resources required
- Memory grids: visual and auditory.
- Examples of adverts taken from magazines, newspapers or video.
- Recordings of television adverts.

Activities
The memory will work better with information that is structured, as opposed to haphazardly arranged. Demonstrate this to the pupils in the following ways:

- Play the game 'I went to the market and bought an apple, banana, cat, doughnut … '. The items are in alphabetical order, so it is possible for all pupils to recall 26 random items because of the alphabetical clues. Further clues will be available if the game is played within a group. A pupil will be able to think, 'G was Clare's letter. What did she say that began with G?'

- Read out a list of unrelated numbers: 1,9,4,5,1,0,6,6,1,8,1,5,1,6,6,5. These would be impossible to remember without imposing some sort of order on them. When they are broken down into famous historical dates they will be easier to remember: 1945, 1066, 1815, 1665.

- Show videos of TV adverts or distribute examples of adverts cut from magazines. Ask the pupils to analyse which adverts are memorable and why. It will become obvious that the memory is stimulated by strong visual images, catchy jingles, simple stories, attractive people, personal interests, music, repetition or humour. Pupils can discuss ways that they can use this to help themselves remember information – see the Pupil Advice Sheet on page 35.

- Link memory to learning style. The learners whose needs are least catered for in the classroom are kinaesthetic learners; they need to 'do' in order to remember effectively, so ensure that some practical activities that support memory are demonstrated. For examples of such practical activities, see 'How to learn MFL vocabulary kinaesthetically' on page 39.

- Create memory aids such as mind maps, card games and mnemonics which will give visually talented pupils an opportunity to shine. The aids can be designed for pupils of the same age or younger children. Use notice boards to display these mind maps or examples of mnemonics to create interest amongst other students.

- Work around the class with each pupil asking another pupil a question, but answering the question set before the last one. Pupils enjoy the ridiculous nature of this activity. It demonstrates clearly that it is necessary to concentrate in order to remember.

    Q. What Day comes after Thursday?

    A. Red.

    Q. Does the sun set in the East or in the West.

    A. Friday.

    Q. Who is captain of the England football squad?

    A. West.

Visual and Auditory Memory Assessment

Informal assessments of auditory and visual memory are useful to demonstrate how the memory works and to pinpoint a pupil's strengths.

Auditory memory

With pupils listening read aloud at two second intervals the following words: cloud, paper, night, mud, but, light, thunder, purpose, but, card, to, red, ship, *EastEnders*, soft, scrap, they, run, cherry, colour, but, itchy, chair, take, corn.

See how many of the words they can write down in two minutes. They then compare lists.

A lot of the words recalled will be from the beginning of the list. Simply because levels of concentration were higher at that point. Unusual words like *EastEnders* will be memorable. Words that can be grouped (for example, cherry, red and colour) and words that were repeated are more likely to have been recalled. Words at the end of the list will be remembered because they were the last heard.

This exercise should demonstrate that memory works best when it is first used, has been recently used, or has been presented with unusual, repeated or linked information. Discuss why it might be useful to know this when learning information for a test. Pupils might suggest that short, regular, revision sessions with lots of repetition and the use of prompts such as mnemonics or memory stories would appear to be an effective way to learn.

Visual memory

Pupils have two minutes to look at the first grid in the appendices (see page 95). Then they turn the grid over and write down from memory as many objects as they can in their correct positions. Allow two minutes for this.

Discuss the different methods used by pupils in this exercise to memorise facts. Work out which strategies are most popular. Examples might include: grouping the pictures into sets, making up short stories or mnemonics, chanting or visualising. Some pupils may not be aware of the advantages of linking information to help with memorising.

Pupils are then given the second memory grid and must try an approach that they have not used before to see if they are more successful. (See Compound Words and Memory Grid 2 in the Appendices)

Some pupils may panic when given this type of task because they have previous experiences of failure. This gives the opportunity to explain the effect of panic on short-term memory, the flight or fight response and how this might affect pupils in tests or exams. It is useful to know how panic blanks out the thinking part of the brain – see Chapter 8 on exam anxiety (page 84)

Note

The memory grids are printed A4 in grayscale in the book but are available as full colour images on A3 sheets printable from the CD-ROM.

Pupil Advice Sheet (Memory)

It is necessary to make an effort to remember. It is easy to remember a friend's phone number, but harder to recall a mathematical equation. It may be easy to take one's mobile out at weekends and keep it safe, but more difficult to remember sports kit for a Games lesson.

Our desire to remember information has a direct effect upon our success with the task.

Memory works best when information is structured, patterned and linked to existing knowledge, we can then make sense of new facts. The more we can understand, the less we have to remember by rote.

However, there is a variety of ways to recall any isolated facts that we need to memorise. It is worth experimenting with several methods to see what works best for you. Everyone will have different preferences.

- We tend to remember items from the beginning or the end of a memory session, so take regular breaks when working in order to create lots of new beginnings and endings.

- The unusual and bizarre are most memorable, so make up your own funny, personal or rude mnemonics. A common trick with mnemonics is to take the first letter of a group of words that you need to memorise and put them into a sentence. For example, to recall the musical scale notation EGBDF, we generally use the sentence **E**very **G**ood **B**oy **D**eserves **F**un.

- Make up short stories to link words or facts together.

- To establish memory triggers, associate names, dates or facts with objects in your room or places you pass on your way to school.

- Use rhythmic poems: 'In fourteen hundred and ninety-two, Columbus sailed the ocean blue'.

- Summarise a quantity of information into a few key words or points. List these words on cards and use them as memory triggers for further detail.

- Some individuals have photographic memories; they can look at information, take a 'photograph' of it in their heads and then recall the image later. This strategy can work for more people when information is converted into a mind map. The colour, illustrations and pattern of a mind map will convert linear information into picture form. It is possible to remember the overall shape of the picture, the key facts and then the supporting detail.

- A variation on the previous idea is visualisation. Make a determined effort to visualise a sequence of events, as if you were creating your own personal video. This could be to support a scientific experiment, an historical event or scenes from an English set book. Run through your video several times: before you go to sleep, when you are in the bath or on the way to school.

- Use all of your senses. Some individuals will remember best when they have been told facts, others when they have seen facts written down. Some people can listen to information that they have taped in order to learn it, while others will remember facts better if they are displayed in a diagram, sketch, flow chart or another visual form. Experiment with lots of methods to see what works best for you.

- Over-learning and repetition are vital. Chant the facts as you walk up and down the stairs; read them aloud over and over again; listen to tapes you have made; test yourself or ask friends to test you on facts written on file cards. Revisit information frequently to keep it fresh in your mind.

- Your memory will not work well when you are tired, have tried to learn too much, have worked for too long without a break, or if you do not understand the information. So look after your health: take regular breaks, eat well, drink plenty of water, exercise and make sure that you get enough sleep.

Listening and Attention

'The true art of memory is the art of attention'. (Dr Johnson)

Pupils must be aware that it is necessary to make the effort to concentrate. Taking an active part in lessons will help with attention.

They must participate fully in lessons, think of questions to ask, join in class discussion, focus on a speaker, look at their face, read their body language and listen carefully to what is being said.

If attention wanders, pupils should try to participate more actively by highlighting or annotating worksheets, by note taking or mind mapping, and by creating flow diagrams, time lines or a sequence of sketches.

Lesson Plan

Learning objective
Pupils to become aware of strategies they can use to develop listening skills and improve their level of attention.

Resources required
- Class texts.

- Video or audio tape of a television or radio news broadcast.

- A selection of detailed pictures from magazines and newspapers or photocopied from books.

Activities

- Read a short extract from a class text and ask pupils to experiment with different ways of listening.

- Read a passage and allow them to jot down notes as you read. Then ask questions relating to the passage.

- Read a passage allowing them to create a mind map of the information as you read. Then ask questions about the text.

- Ask pupils to visualise the sequence of information as you read, making it into a video in their heads. Then ask related questions.

- Read the questions that you will ask first to allow pupils to tune in to the key information. Read the passage, then ask the questions.

Practising these different routines will give pupils an idea of different listening strategies and what will suit them best.

Read other passages and explain that you will be asking comprehension questions about key information afterwards. Pupils can then choose which strategies to use.

Tape or video radio or television news broadcasts for groups or pairs of pupils to listen to or to watch – they are not allowed to take notes and so have to make an effort to listen carefully. Then ask questions about the broadcasts. What information was remembered accurately and what was forgotten? Discuss why this might be.

Allow pupils two minutes to look at a detailed picture then they must turn the picture over and ask each other questions about the illustration. Points are won or lost depending upon the accuracy of their answers.

Repeat the activity with a second picture. This time they are allowed to copy the illustration on to a separate sheet of blank paper and talk quietly to themselves about each part of the picture as they draw it. 'The man with the black hair is standing in the right corner of the room. He is looking out of the window at a woman in the garden. You can only see the woman's shoulders. She is wearing ... '. Then they answer questions. This will demonstrate that memory is more effective after multi-sensory input: looking, drawing, talking, listening.

Read the pupils a list of 4, 5, 6 or 7 objects as appropriate to age and ability level. Re-read the list omitting one object. Pupils then have to identify the missing object. The list could be of linked words: apple, lemon, banana, orange, grape and strawberry, or random words: tree, carpet, butterfly, ship, woollen and elephant. Encourage pupils to use visualisation techniques to remember the objects.

Pupils complete a diagram from oral instruction. The pupils listen as a sequence of instructions is read out, then pick up their pencils and follow the directions. The length and type of instructions would be suitable to the groups' ability level and ages. Their attention, and therefore their memory, will improve with practice.

For example, for Year 7/8:

- *Instruction 1* Turn your paper into landscape position. Write your name in capitals in the middle of the paper and draw three small triangles in a horizontal line on the top left hand corner of the page.

- *Instruction 2* Underline your name, then draw three lines crossing the page from the top left hand corner to the bottom right hand corner. Make one line wavy and two straight.

Pupil Advice Sheet (Concentration)

- Know your own levels of attention. If you find it difficult to talk and listen at the same time, try not to be drawn into conversation by your friends in class.

- Watch the teacher's face as he or she speaks.

- If other pupils in your class distract you, try not to sit near them. Some people find it easier to sit at the front of the class with their back to friends. Others prefer to sit at the back of the class where it is possible to see everything that is going on, rather than to speculate about what might be happening behind you.

- Ask if you can open a window to keep the room well ventilated. You are more likely to stay alert if there is a good supply of fresh air.

- Take a break as you listen: stretch your legs out under the desk, wriggle your fingers, lift and hold your feet off the floor to the count of ten. Any exercise like this will get the blood moving round your body and oxygen to your brain.

- Participate actively in the lesson. Think of questions to ask, join in discussions and take notes. Even if you are not asked a question directly, think of how you would have answered questions directed at other pupils.

- It can help to run through the previous lesson in your head on your way to the classroom; then you will be tuned in to the subject as soon as the lesson starts.

- Be determined to concentrate. If teachers see that you are making an effort to concentrate, they are more likely to want to help you.

When working alone:

- Many individuals find it hard to concentrate for any length of time when working by themselves, so use a variety of approaches to add novelty, involve all your senses and keep yourself motivated.

- Alternate passive activities like reading with something more active: create a mind map for an essay plan or a set of question and answer cards for a test.

- Be aware of when you work most effectively during the day. Save the work that you find hardest for that time of day when your levels of concentration are higher.

- Make sure you have everything you need before you start work to minimise distractions: turn off your mobile, open a window, have a drink to hand and shut the door.

- If you are reading, try to read as quickly as possible. You will have to concentrate more.

- If you suddenly remember something else you have to do, try not to be distracted: make a note of it and then refocus. Sometimes it can help to set aside time each day to think about the things that are troubling you. If you begin to worry about them, you can then say to yourself 'I'm thinking about that after lunch', and can then get on with the task in hand.

- If your mind is wandering, try saying aloud to yourself 'Stop. You must think about this'. It may be enough to refocus your attention.

- Make activities short and concentrated. Use a stopwatch to time yourself: 'I will read and make notes on this chapter for 20 minutes, then I will make a mind map of the information for 10 minutes, then I will listen to my revision tape while I have a bath for 15 minutes'. It will be easier for you to focus if you know that the time you are spending on an activity is limited.

- If you lose concentration and are unable to get back on task, do not feel guilty. This is not a disaster. Allow yourself a break: have a drink, eat a sandwich, watch TV for 30 minutes or tidy your CDs – then come back and start again.

- A break that involves some form of physical activity is best. Walking around the block for 10 minutes is perfect: it combines physical exercise with fresh air.

How to Learn MFL Vocabulary Kinaesthetically

One of the problems experienced by pupils studying languages in school is remembering large amounts of unfamiliar vocabulary. Pupils need to be shown ways to learn vocabulary.

It is worth pointing out that simply talking about and deciding how to retain vocabulary mean that close attention is paid to the words and so memorising will be easier.

Most memorising strategies will be transferable to other subjects. Time spent thinking about ways to remember information is never time wasted.

It is most effective for pupils to learn vocabulary in short, regular sessions rather than revise long lists in one attempt. The latter is boring and can lead to confusion and panic.

To make vocabulary lists appear more manageable, teach pupils to follow these initial steps:

- Eliminate all vocabulary that is already known. The task immediately becomes less onerous.

- Divide the remaining words into those that are nearly known and those that are unknown. Words that are nearly known can be revised a few times with flash cards – see the Pupil Advice Sheet (How to learn MFL vocabulary) on pages 43–4.

- Any remaining vocabulary will need targeting.

Approximately one third of all pupils will have kinaesthetic learning preferences. The younger the pupil, the more attractive a practical approach to learning will be to them, so it is important that lessons have a generous kinaesthetic component.

Games provide the perfect classroom activity for kinaesthetic learners, but will also match other learners' needs. Games necessitate:

- Working with others.

- Moving about and handling practical apparatus.

- Everyone to be involved.

- Regular changes of activity.

- Discussion.

They also give the opportunity for the over-learning that is essential for quick recall of vocabulary without the drudgery of pencil and paper work.

Lesson Plan

Learning objective
Pupils will learn how to revise MFL vocabulary through games.

Resources required
- Blank cards for games and flash cards.

- MFL dictionaries.

- Sheets of A3 paper.

- Dice.
- A whiteboard or OHP.
- Prompt sheet.

Activities

Link cards   To be used as a whole-class or group activity. The game can be adapted to suit a variety of ages and ability levels.

Provide each small group with a set of blank pieces of card, 7cms by 4cms being a perfect size. The group lays the cards out end to end. They then draw a line down the middle of each card and put a MFL word from their vocabulary list on the right hand side of the card and the English equivalent on the left hand side of the next card. When they reach the end of the line, the word on the right hand side of the last card must match the word on the left hand side of the first card to complete the loop.

If the pupils make their own cards, they will target those words that they are finding difficult. Thinking about which words to include and how to illustrate them will provide useful over-learning.

A combination of words, phrases, illustrations or cartoons can be used depending on the ages and ability levels of the group.

The cards can be shuffled and played as dominoes by individuals, pairs or small groups.

If one set comprises of an adequate number of cards for the whole class to use, the game can be an oral activity for all the pupils. The class is timed as the loop is completed; they then try to cut back that time. The cards should be shuffled and redistributed after each game.

Treasure hunt   Pupils work individually, in pairs or in small groups to create a map of a French/Italian/Spanish/German town on a sheet of A3 paper. (The game can be adapted from a town to the inside of a home, school or shop, on the beach, at the zoo and so forth.) Pupils can include a selection of landmarks, such as a church, school, cinema, swimming pool, railway station, railway line, bridge, river, motorway, hospital and supermarket. Other features can be added as appropriate: parks with ponds, play areas, flowerbeds, paths, wooded areas and streams.

The pupils have ten minutes to work through a prompt sheet, reminding each other of the relevant vocabulary for towns and how to give directions. They then choose six places to bury a box of treasure and make a note of the six spots. Each individual, pair or small group then joins with another individual, pair or group and, using their map, tries to guide the other pair to the treasure sites using instructions in the relevant language; for example *'Prenez la première rue a gauche, continuez jusqu'a l'Hôtel de Ville, et puis allez droit jusqu'a la gare. Prenez la première rue a gauche après la gare, traversez la rue et le treasure est dans le jardin public'.*

Acting it out   Divide the class into small groups. Each group is given six French/German/Spanish words from a current vocabulary list. They must use these words in a short, two minute play. They have ten minutes to translate the vocabulary, work on a script and ensure that all the words are used in a natural and appropriate way. The rest of the class have a list of the words that different groups have been given. While one group performs their play, the rest of the class must listen for these words. Other pupils stand up when they think they have heard a word. If the first person to stand up is correct they score a point for their team, if they are incorrect, they lose a point.

Dice game   The pupils work in pairs or small groups. Each pair or small group has a set of cards, which they number from 1 to 12. On the back of the cards they write a word or a phrase that they are finding difficult to remember. They then take it in turns to throw two die: the number that is thrown determines which card is turned over. Younger pupils can put the word or phrase into a sentence; older pupils can build up a story sentence by sentence, with the word or phrase on each card being incorporated into the next sentence.

Miming vocabulary   Working in small groups, pupils select a list of 20 words that they find difficult to remember and write them on cards. The cards are shuffled between the pupils, who take turns at miming to the others the word on their card. The other pupils take it in turns to identify, translate and spell the word.

Comics   Each pupil creates a story in cartoon form using a specified number of words from a vocabulary list. Each story must involve two or more characters depending upon the number of participants. The class is organised into groups to act out each other's cartoons.

Action songs   For example, try 'Mein Hut der hat drei Ecken' which is similar to 'In a Cottage in a Wood'.

Different action songs can be designated to different groups, who then take it in turns to demonstrate and teach the song to the rest of the class. The songs will be as comical and ridiculous as possible to reinforce the 'hard to remember' vocabulary.

Hide and Seek   Pupils each prepare their own set of flash cards with the English word on one side and the MFL word on the other. They time themselves as they run through the cards. The aim here is to get quicker each time the set is completed. They can then test a partner.

Chains   Create a chain of words in alphabetical order all linked to the same topic. 'I packed my suitcase and in it I put an anorak, a beach towel, a cap ...' (clothing). 'I went to the market and bought an apple, banana, carrot, donut, egg ... ' (food).

Quiz bingo   Give each pupil, pair or small group a bingo 'card' with 20 vocabulary questions written in each square. You could write and photocopy these, or pupils could write the questions for each other. Depending on the ages or abilities of the group, the questions could be ones that they could answer from memory or that need a degree of research, perhaps from a class text, vocabulary list or on a CD. The pupils can play against each other within a pair, small group or against the rest of the class.

The first person or group to answer the questions and cover four corners or a line wins.

The Weakest Link, Blockbusters, Mastermind, A Question of Sport   There are many television game shows that can be adapted for pairs, groups or as a whole class to revise vocabulary. For example, in *Blockbusters* a grid filled with single letters is put up on the OHP. The class works in two teams to cross the grid either vertically or horizontally. What 'c' is a type of Spanish boat? What 'd' is a type of vegetable in German? The first team to cross the grid wins.

Beat the teacher/other pupils   The teacher or a pupil reads a passage or puts up an overhead of a text. The passage or text includes a set number of deliberate errors that the pupils have to spot. There could be ten spelling, vocabulary or grammatical errors, graded in difficulty according to the ability levels and ages of the group.

Test the other half   The class revises the vocabulary from a topic or module and then divides into groups. Each team writes questions for the other groups to answer. The teacher acts as scorekeeper.

Pupil Advice Sheet (How to Learn MFL Vocabulary)

Every individual will have different ways to do this. Try several approaches and see what works best for you. If you do try, but then decide against an approach, you will not have wasted your time. Just thinking about how to learn the vocabulary in a different way will have helped you to retain some of the words.

The first thing you must do is prune the amount of vocabulary to be learnt into a list of essentials: this will ensure that the exercise is manageable. Target those vital but tricky words.

- Write out six to ten words that you are finding hard to remember on a large sheet of paper, draw pictures or illustrations next to the words and blu-tack the paper on the wall or ceiling of your bedroom. Underline any unusual parts of the word that might act as a memory prompt. Study the posters carefully when you are in bed, then close you eyes and try to recall their content.

- Record words, their spellings and their meanings, on tape, then listen to the tapes in the bath, on the bus, as you walk to school or are in bed. The vocabulary will fix itself in your brain like the words of an irritating song. The best time to learn in this way is at night just before you go to sleep, when your brain is more relaxed and receptive. As you sleep your brain will order and sort out the vocabulary for you.

- Write out the word over and over again in different styles of writing: slanting forwards or backwards, in bubble writing, upright or in capitals. Use different coloured and sized pens and pencils. Say the word as you write it. Shut your eyes and write it. Write the word in the air. Write the word with your left and then with your right hand. Soon the word will flow automatically from your hand in the same way that you write your name.

- Try spell checkers. Hand-held spell checkers often have different 'chips' for foreign spellings. Some have games that will help you learn the vocabulary.

- Test yourself with flash cards. Write the English word on one side with an illustration and the foreign word on the other. Test yourself or ask family or friends to test you. Initially put the cards in the front section of a box file, and run through all of the cards once on a daily basis. Tick each card when you remember the word correctly. When the word has been ticked three times, move it from the front section back into the next section of the box file. Continue to test yourself and when the cards have another three ticks, move them into the third section of the file. By moving the cards like this, you can see the progress you are making. Whenever you revise the words, always start with the cards in the front section of the file, and then you are targeting the words that you find most difficult to remember.

  It is easier to remember the English word from the MFL word, so work from MFL to English until you feel confident in your knowledge, and then turn the cards round and translate from the English word to the MFL word.

- School libraries, public libraries and bookshops stock attractively presented books designed for younger children. You can use these for revision at home. They are useful because they explain language and spellings in ways that will be easier to understand. Some of these series have tapes to listen to alongside the books so that you can look at the spelling as you hear the word pronounced. Ask your teacher if your school has any of these.

- Some publishers produce interactive CD-ROMS linked to MFL syllabuses. These can be useful if you learn in a visual way. Your school, a public library and bookshops will stock them.

- Make little cards with foreign words and pictures on and blu-tack them around your house: on the back of your door, the phone, a mirror, where you hang your jacket, on the top of the TV or the fridge. Every time that you see the card you will have a visual reminder of the word. The location of the card will help to prompt your recall: if you need to remind yourself of the verb 'wash', shut your eyes and imagine that you are standing in front of the prompt card by the mirror in the bathroom.

- Look for associations and links between foreign and English words; for example *avoir* = to 'ave.

- Make up your own dictionary with vocabulary grouped under appropriate headings. Rewrite the lists, rearrange their order, and draw pictures or annotated cartoons. The more you organise and restructure this material, the more familiar it will become.

- Walk up and down the stairs repeating the words in English and then the other language. One syllable for each step. Shout out and then whisper the words in an exaggerated accent.

- You may be able to make up mnemonics as we do in order to remember English spellings. 'I will be your friend to the end' = friend. 'Big Elephants Can Always Understand Small Elephants' = because.

Organisation

For disorganised individuals effective personal organisation can seem an overwhelming challenge, but a few simple routines can make a substantial improvement and save an extraordinary amount of time.

Pupils with poor organisational skills often have family members with similar problems; they may be able to pass on useful strategies. Pupils could ask peers, adults and teachers to share their experiences; this may make others more understanding, whereas constantly borrowing (and losing) equipment will make individuals unpopular with family, friends and teachers alike.

Pupil Advice Sheet (General Organisation)

- Try to stay in control of your workload. Carry a notebook, diary or a Filo-fax in your bag. If you have a good idea at an odd moment, write it down immediately before you forget it.

- Use these notebooks to make lists of things to be done. Review the lists daily, put stars by those activities requiring priority action, delete activities where action has been taken, and write down any new tasks.

- Keep daily schedules and timetables in several places: desks, bags and on bedroom doors or walls.

- Clearly label or mark your folders for each subject so that you always pick up the correct file even if you are in a hurry. Use coloured paper in files to separate topics. Sections at the back of the files could include lists of formulae, definitions and key word spellings.

- Use too many files rather than too few.

- If you use a computer, get into the habit of backing up all your work and labelling discs clearly. It is easy to think that you will be able to remember obscure titles for your work, but you won't.

- Always keep everything in the same place: 'My keys are always in the pocket at the front of my bag, my trainers are always in my locker, my pencil case is always in the bottom of my bag, and my protractor is always in my blue Maths case'. When you get into automatic routines, your equipment will always be in the same place, even if you were distracted when you put it away.

- Spend a few minutes each day tidying and sorting out your desk, your workspace at home and your bag. Use pots for pens, Tippex, Sellotape and pencils, boxes for compasses, protractors and calculators and trays for spare paper and worksheets.

- Break down large assignments into smaller more manageable tasks, and set yourself short-term targets: 'Today I'll write out the introduction to the essay, tomorrow I'll get a few books to collect ideas from and at the weekend I'll draw out some graphs'. If you work in this way, you will be able to see your progress and not panic.

- List contents, subject specific spellings, homework times, dates for coursework, on the inside cover of each file as soon as you are given them.

- Organise your school bag the previous evening. You will then have time to find your football socks, borrow your brother's calculator or ask your parents to fill in permission slips.

- Keep spare sets of equipment in your bags, your desk or locker, as well as at home.

- Transparent pencil cases are useful; you can check the contents easily.

- ICT can be useful for planning and organising work. Some pupils find electronic organisers a boon.

Pupil Advice Sheet (Organising Homework)

- Always note down any homework as soon as it is given.

- Work regularly and at a steady pace to avoid work piling up. Working in guilty bursts is tiring and de-motivating.

- Run through and prioritise homework each evening: 'This work has to be in at register, I will need to get started on this tomorrow, but I can leave that reading until the weekend'.

- Write the date that work is due in your diary. Then work backwards from that date filling in other dates. 'Hand essay in on November 11th, proofread essay on the 7th, final write up of essay on the weekend of the 30th October', and so on. Pacing work backwards like this will avoid last minute panics.

- Organise a space for yourself at home with a collection of spare equipment.

- Keep friends' phone numbers available in case you have questions about homework.

- Be self-disciplined. Set yourself timed work slots and do not use avoidance strategies.

- Allow yourself rewards for sustained effort: 'If I write out these notes for 30 minutes, then I can watch *EastEnders*'.

6
Writing

Note Taking: Linear Notes and Mind Mapping

Many pupils have difficulty in this area and benefit from being shown how to note take.

It is not always obvious to students who are unfamiliar with subject matter, which facts are important and which are not. They will either write down everything or nothing at all.

Other pupils will have problems with the multi-tasking required by note taking: spelling, presentation, listening and understanding.

Lesson Plan

Learning objective
Pupils will have an increased understanding of the variety of note-taking strategies available to them.

Resources required
- A whiteboard or an OHP.

- Highlighters or coloured pencils.

- Tapes of television or radio news broadcasts.

Activities
- One of the pupils reads a passage from a class text, while the teacher models note taking on the whiteboard or OHP. Alternatively, the teacher note takes from a piece of text on the OHP. As the teacher writes, she explains what she is doing and why. This has the additional advantage of raising staff awareness of how to give clear, precise notes.

Key points to demonstrate:

1 How to summarise text into key points. Look for names, headings, dates and places.

2 How to look at the introduction and summary of the passage to work out the main ideas of a text.

3 How to recognise redundant material such as repetitions, supporting detail or personal comments.

4 How to use mind mapping as an alternative recording method.

5 How to spell words phonetically and look up correct spellings later.

6 How to use diagrams and drawings to simplify ideas. A picture can say a thousand words.

7 How to look for ways to convert information into lists or record it under bullet points.

8 How to use common abbreviations: etc, et al., i.e., Dec, &, +, Tues, x, =, <, and *. Think text messaging.

9 How to make up your own shorthand, perhaps by using the first letters of words: diff, Parl, disadv, prob, nat.

- The class watches or listens to a news broadcast taped from the television or radio and then writes down the key points from each news item. Tell them to focus on the main facts: the place where the event occurred, the names of the individuals involved and any dates mentioned.

  Pupils then compare notes in pairs or small groups, checking that the main points have been recorded accurately. Each set of pupils gives feedback to the rest of the class on a different news items using their notes as memory prompts. Points are scored for information remembered and can be gained from other groups for information omitted. The complexity of activity can be increased for older students and as the pupils gain experience in note taking.

- The teacher can demonstrate some of the many uses of mind mapping: in note taking from text, planning work, brain storming, or as a revision strategy. For example:

  CLASSIFICATION OF ANIMALS – (linear form)

  VERTEBRATE (backbone)

  INVERTEBRATES (no backbone)

  Invertebrates – spiders and insects

  1 Spiders have 0 wings, a 2-part body and 8 legs.

  2 Insects have 1 set of antennae, a 3-part body, 2 wings and 6 legs.

Pupils can convert this linear list into a simple mind map to illustrate how the information is linked and give a visual pattern to assist memory.

Pupils can then practise making mind maps from the Pupil Advice Sheet (Note taking) – see pages 52–3. Stress the use of numbers, upper and lower case letters, underlining, grouping of points, abbreviations, highlighting, diagrams and arrows to link common ideas.

It may be worth pointing out to pupils that coloured file paper is easier on the eye than white paper when taking notes for long periods. Coloured paper also makes the sorting of notes into topics easier.

If an individual's note-taking skills are dire, allow them to use duplicating paper. They can ask friends if they would mind duplicating a copy of their notes, thus allowing the

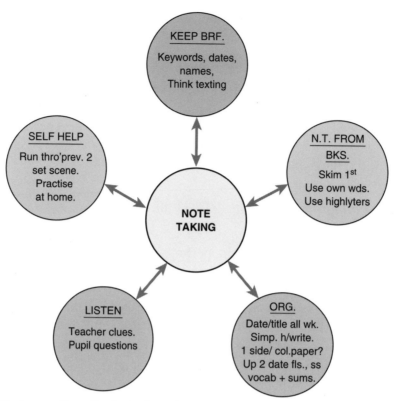

Figure 6.1   Mind map of pupil advice sheet (note taking)

pupil with the difficulty to concentrate on mind mapping an overview or on listening for understanding. After the lesson both pupils can read through the duplicated notes together to check their understanding.

Pupil Advice Sheet (Mind Mapping)

The aim of a mind map is to convert written text or information organised in a linear fashion into a visual format. A mind map cuts down on the risk of over recording as only key words and points are used.

How to create a mind map

- Select a text.

- Highlight relevant key words from the text.

- Group these words into sets.

- Take a sheet of paper and turn it to landscape position.

- Write the title of the text or draw a picture to represent the title in the middle of the page.

- Draw one line coming out of the central picture or title for each set of key words.

- Use different colours for each line.

- Write the most important word at the end of each line.

- Write other related key words on other lines radiating from each important keyword.

- Use lots of space to keep the total image clear.

- Add sketches and illustrations to make the image as visual as possible. The mind map does not have to be artistic or neat, it is for your own use.

- Use capital letters, different coloured pens, highlighting and underlining to make points visually clear.

Pupil Advice Sheet (Note Taking)

Note taking from talks and presentations

- Think about the content of the previous lesson before the session starts, so that your brain is tuned in to the subject.

- Date and title every piece of paper.

- Listen for your teacher giving verbal clues: 'Now this is really important', 'So, in summary', or 'The opposite argument would be true in the case of ...'. Whatever information follows will be key.

- Look at the person who is talking. If they are speaking too quickly, ask them to slow down.

- Listen to other pupils. They may ask about information that you haven't understood. Do not be afraid to ask for clarification.

- Use your own codes: ring dates, box names, number key points, highlight legislation, underline place names, print examples in capital letters.

- Experiment with making notes in different styles: mind mapping, linear notes or diagrams.

- Write key words and key points only. Do not be tempted to try to write everything down, you will be overwhelmed and lose heart. Take notes as if you were writing a text message.

- Use abbreviations: eg, etc, =, +, &, Shkp = Shakespeare, Parlnt = Parliament, elct = electricity.

- Keep your writing simple. Cut back on excessive loops and fancy swirls on letters.

- Put a question mark in the margin against information you are not clear about and ask for clarification later.

- Write on every other line. This will make your notes seem clearer and leave you space to add correct spellings and explanations later. A double margin could be used in the same way.

- Some pupils use one side of the page and leave the reverse for revision notes and summaries. If you use the back of the previous page for updating, you will have a two-page spread: the left page for summaries, key words and points added later, and the right page with your original notes on.

- Practise taking notes from radio or television news broadcasts.

- Organise your notes after each session.

- Keep a set of file cards with subject specific vocabulary and definitions in the front of each file to check on the meanings of unfamiliar words.

- If you know that you are going to miss a lesson, ask a friend if they would mind if you photocopied their notes.

Note taking from books and other texts

- When taking notes from a book, check its publication date to ensure that the information is current.

- Always record the page number to refer back to if necessary. This sort of recording is a good habit to develop; completing a bibliography will be required of older students.

- Use postcards as a bookmark and for notes. Jot brief notes down on the card as you read: when the card is full, file it and start a new card. After reading the text, read through your cards, highlight the key information and write a summary out on a side of A4.

- When note taking from a borrowed textbook, photocopy the necessary pages and highlight the information on your photocopy. Note down the title of the book, author, publisher and date of publication on the reverse of the photocopy for reference.

- Skim read a passage before you start making notes. It might not contain any relevant information.

- Read the passage, and then write the information out in your own words to check your understanding.

Essays

Stress to pupils that it is worth spending time planning an essay to ensure that it is coherent and well balanced.

Lesson Plan

Learning objective
Pupils will have an increased understanding of basic essay structure.

Resources required
- A whiteboard or an OHP.
- Photocopied copies of exemplar essays.

Activities
The teacher models one or more of the following approaches to essay planning as appropriate to the age of the pupils.

The Questions Approach: who, what, which, when, where and why? This approach is useful for structuring a descriptive essay, for example, 'My Perfect Holiday', or as an exercise for demonstrating the use of mind mapping as a planning tool.

- Why? Why did you choose to go there? Recommendation, brochure or habit?
- Where? Where did you go? Coast, city or countryside?
- Who? Who went with you? Who did you meet while you were there?
- Which? Which part of the holiday did you enjoy most?
- When? When did you go there? Half-term, as a young child, last year?
- What? What did you do? Skiing, swimming, sunbathing, sightseeing or hiking?

Mind maps to think of and to organise ideas: as in the Questions Approach to essay writing, or group arguments for and against a statement.

Linear plans to sequence ideas or topics: introduction, characters, events, reaction, resolution and conclusion.

- Pupils work in pairs looking at the comments the teacher has made about their partner's previous essays to see if there is a recurring theme: a strong introduction, a good use of quotes, not enough detail included, not answering the question set or a weak sequencing of facts. Then they try to work out how that specific essay could be improved or why it is good.
- Pupils examine a photocopy of an essay from a previous year group in small groups. Each group highlights a few good points about the essay: clear structure, relevant detail, good conclusion and imaginative use of language. The groups then look for

areas where improvement could be made, for example: better grammar, a stronger introduction or more appropriate use of quotes. The points could then be discussed as a class.

- The teacher presents each pair with a short essay, photocopied on to card and cut up into ten separate sections. The pupils have to reassemble the sections into a whole and justify the order they chose. This will clarify the importance of sequence in an essay.

- Terminology: have a quiz on the meanings of essay vocabulary. Essay key words and meanings can be photocopied on to card and then cut up into separate piles of words and definitions. Pupils then have to reassemble the correct pairs.

1 Apply = Explain how an idea or concept would work through the use of examples.

2 Compare = Show similarities and differences between two or more things.

3 Contrast = Highlight the differences between two or more things.

4 Discuss = Provide a detailed description including arguments for and against.

5 Explain = Tell why something happened.

6 Justify = Give arguments to support your statement.

7 Outline = Condense a topic under main headings with subheadings used as support.

8 Relate = Show connections between ideas and concepts.

9 State = Offer main points without discussion.

10 Summarise = Bring knowledge together with an emphasis on the main points.

Revise the use of these key words, and give pupils a copy of the definitions.

Pupil Advice Sheet (Essay Writing)

It is vital to spend some time planning your essay. The more time spent in planning, the less time spent in correcting.

When writing the essay

1 Understand the task.

   Precisely what are you being asked to do? Underline any key words in the title. Write out the title on a separate piece of paper and leave it in front of you as you write. This will help to ensure you keep to the point.

2 Assemble the resources you will need.

   Collect together your notes, relevant textbooks and articles. Remember to record page numbers in case you need to refer back to a book for information.

3 Use these resources efficiently.

   Read through the resources carefully. Make summary notes of key points.

4 Make your plan and first draft.

   Order all of the key points and the detail supporting each one. This could be in the form of linear notes or a mind map.

   Brainstorm all of your ideas, sort them by colour coding: underline arguments for in red, arguments against in green, useful points for the conclusion in blue, and so forth.

   Cut up your notes into sections and rearrange them into a more logical order or use the cut and paste facility on a computer.

5 Write the essay.

   - In the introduction, refer back to the title in order to focus your thoughts. The introductory paragraph tells the reader what the essay will be about.

   - The central portion of the essay will include a paragraph for each of the main points you wish to discuss. Your arguments should be clearly stated, with strongest arguments at the beginning and end of this section, and weaker arguments in the middle.

   - In the conclusion summarise the main themes of your argument. In the last sentence refer back to the title again.

   - Read the essay aloud to ensure it makes sense. If someone else is happy to listen as you do this, they can check for overall meaning. Any questions that they ask about the content will pinpoint areas for you to add clarification.

Word-processing can make the organisation of an essay easier because of the cut and paste facility. Thinking can be separated from writing; you can get your ideas down and correct sequence, spelling and grammar later.

Read through your teacher's comments on previous pieces of work. You may be making the same mistakes over and over again.

Ask friends who get good marks for work, if you could read their essays. Look at the essays carefully and read the teacher's comments.

Definitions of Essay Vocabulary

Understanding the words used in essay questions will help you understand what you are being asked to do.

Analyse = Examine the main ideas in detail.

Comment on = Give your opinion.

Compare = Show similarities and differences between items.

Contrast = Show differences between items.

Define = State the meaning precisely.

Discuss = Write about the most important aspects of the topic.

Enumerate = List.

Evaluate = Give good and bad points about a subject.

Explain = Give details about how and why.

Examine = Look closely at the information and draw conclusions.

Illustrate = Give examples or comparisons to make information clear and specific.

Interpret = Give the meaning using examples and comments.

Outline = Give brief notes of the most important points.

Predict = Use information to say what will happen as a result.

State = A brief answer giving basic facts.

Summarise = List all the main points.

Trace = Follow the main order of different stages in an event.

Proof Reading

As we read we glance at and absorb whole words rather than checking the sequence of the letters within a word.

In tihs psagsae eervy wrod wtih mroe tahn trhee ltteres has had the odrer of the ltretes in the mdldie of the wrod chgaend. The frsit and lsat lttrees rmiaen the smae. Hwveeor, the reedar is stlil albe to mkae snsee of the psasgae.

We see what we want to see, so it makes sense to leave work for a day or two before proof reading for spelling.

Sometimes it is suggested that a pupil reads backwards through their work to check for spelling errors. This is both time consuming and tedious. If absolute accuracy is essential in a piece of work, the same pupil would find it less frustrating to ask a friend or family member to check for obvious errors.

Pupils should however read aloud to check for sense and flow. Discuss the different interpretations that could be drawn from the following sentences and rephrase them into a clearer form:

- Our dog eats anything and likes children.
- The minister strolled among the guests eating their sandwiches.
- There will be a meeting on motorbikes in Room 10.
- We had 50 pairs of Wellington boots on our hands.
- The woman saw the girl jumping through a hole in the fence.

Pupil Advice Sheet (Proof Reading)

- Try to separate your writing from your proof reading. Get your ideas down first without worrying about spelling, grammar or the order of your arguments. Come back to your work later to organise and check it.

- If your work is word-processed rather than hand written, it will be easier to read, spell check and re-order.

- We tend to read what we hope we have written, so leave your work until the following day before checking it through and you will be more likely to spot any errors.

- It is often suggested that proof reading for spelling mistakes is easier if you go through the passage from the end to the beginning. With longer pieces of work this can be very tedious, so ask a friend or member of your family to check for spelling errors.

- To check for sense and punctuation, read the passage aloud. This may be easier if you record it on tape, and then listen back to it to concentrate on checking accuracy and flow.

Spelling

A lack of confidence with spelling will affect the fluency of a pupil's written work. If a student is aware that their spelling is weak, they will avoid using adult words and phrases and continue to use simple vocabulary that may not reflect their maturing thought processes.

Most pupils can improve their spelling by adopting a few simple strategies. For older pupils it is important that alternative techniques are discussed. Encourage these pupils to word process their work and to use their computer's spellchecker. Demonstrate how to use hand-held spellcheckers. Read through the pupil advice sheet together and discuss any strategies that they might find specifically useful.

Lesson Plan

Learning objective
Pupils will identify ways to increase the accuracy of their spelling.

Resources required
- Writing equipment.

- Whiteboard.

- Photocopies of 'Our Queer Language' (see page 62)

Activities
- Ask pupils to spell ten words that are acknowledged to be difficult. Ensure that the pupils realise that the exercise is not to try to catch them out, but to demonstrate how confusing English spelling can be. The list will be dependent on their ages and ability levels. An example for Key Stage 3 pupils might be: accommodation, necessary, separate, environment, friends, Mediterranean, occasion, temperature, Caribbean and Arctic.

- Ask pupils to work in pairs. They choose three words from the list above that they spelt incorrectly or were unsure of. Teach them the following routine:

  1 Write the word down carefully and examine its pattern closely.

  2 Take a photograph of the word in your head. Shut your eyes to make sure that the image is clear.

  3 Trace the word in the air with your finger.

  4 While your eyes are shut, spell the word aloud backwards (that is, the word 'friend' would be spelt d-n-e-i-r-f). Your partner checks that your spelling is correct.

  5 Write the word down with the hand that you do not normally use for writing.

  6 Write the word in capital letters or bubble writing.

  7 Write the word with your eyes closed, saying each letter name as you write it: 'F,R,I,E,N,D spells friend'.

  8 This routine can be used to learn the spellings of tricky words. It ensures that pupils think about the individual letters that make up a word and note the order of those letters within it.

- Distribute the Pupil Advice Sheet (spelling) - See page 63. Work through some of the spelling strategies and practise the techniques: for example, mnemonics, spelling rules, word families and key words. Discuss those which you find useful as an adult and those that different pupils use.

- Many pupils have confusions over homophones. These are words that have the same sound (would/wood, break/brake, sea/see). How many homophones can pupils write in a minute? Can they put two homophones into one sensible sentence to show the difference between the words? How many homophones can they put into one sentence: for example 'Eye will meat yew next weakened two bye ewe a knew pear of genes'? (See Homophones in Appendices)

- Distribute printable copies from the CD Rom of 'Our Queer Language': The English language has absorbed words from a variety of cultures and spellings of these can appear irregular. Each pupil goes through their photocopy highlighting visual/auditory mismatches: for example, true, sew, few, verse, worse and horse.

- Ask pupils to research the origins of some English spellings with dictionaries or on the Internet. Examples could include: veranda, salary, canter, harem, bazaar, impersonal, macaroni, yacht, bayonet and port. When pupils develop an interest in words and their origins, spellings can appear more logical.

- Such books as *POSH and Other Language Myths* (2004) by Michael Quinion and *Accomodating Brocolli in the Cemetary* (2004) by Vivian Cook explore the roots of vocabulary and language. These publications could be used to stimulate pupil interest in the subject.

- Try mnemonic competitions. Each pupil designs a visual mnemonic for a tricky subject-specific word: thermometer, equilibrium, organisms, temperature, vacuum, resistance – or for two homophones. Use notice boards to display examples of spelling mnemonics to promote interest amongst pupils. Present photocopies of the best examples in a book for younger pupils.

OUR QUEER LANGUAGE

When the English tongue we speak,

Why is break not rhymed with freak?

Will you tell me why it's true?

We say sew but likewise and few?

And the maker of the verse

Cannot cap his horse with worse?

Beard sounds not the same as heard,

Cord is different from word,

Cow is cow but low is low,

Shoe is never rhymed with foe,

Think of hose and whose and lose,

And think of goose and yet of choose,

Think of comb and tomb and bomb,

Doll and roll and home and some,

And since pay is rhymed with say,

Why not paid with said, I pray?

We have blood and food and good,

Wherefore done and gone and lone?

Is there any reason known?

And, in short, it seems to me

Sounds and letters disagree.

(Lord Cromer, 1841–1917)

Pupil Advice Sheet (Spelling)

- Use mnemonics or memory prompts. 'There is a rat in separate'. 'A secretary can keep a secret'. 'I am in Parliament'. 'A committee has as many members as possible: two 'm's, two 't's and two 'e's.

- Be aware of how words link into families: the word 'garden' is in gardener, gardening, gardened. 'Sign' appears to be an irregular spelling, but will seem more logical if linked with signal or signature.

- Try to learn about suffixes and prefixes: appoint, disappoint, disappointed, disappointment, disappointing. This sort of knowledge will cut back on such errors as imeasureable and unecessary.

- Count the number of syllables in a word to make sure that you don't shorten the spelling, for example, choc/o/late rather than choc/late.

- Pronounce words carefully: environment rather than enviroment, Arctic as opposed to Artic.

- Use a bookmark with useful spellings clearly written on it. These should be those words that you have problems spelling. Keep the bookmark in your pencil case.

- Look for patterns in words: nudge, bridge, sludge, fudge, badge and dodge. Fright, slight, bright, might, knight and midnight.

- Make sure that you can spell common key words: for example, when, but, have, they, said. Thirty of these small words account for approximately a third of everything we write.

- Say the word as you write it. Exaggerate the pronunciation in you head: Wed-nes-day, Feb-ru-ary, E-G-Y-P-T.

- Keep a personal dictionary of corrections of your frequent errors, and refer to it.

- Look at a word carefully, and then make a photograph of it in your head. Imagine the word written in different colours on different coloured backgrounds and choose the best image to remember.

- Word-processing can help with spelling. Some kinaesthetic learners can remember the 'feel' of the word through the sequence of letters on the keyboard.

- Ask teachers to provide spelling lists for topics: Electricity, World War 2, Volcanoes and Respiration. Keep the lists in the front of your book or file and use them.

- If you make minor spelling errors, practise working with a dictionary.

- Look for words within words: spit in hospital, fat/her, cap/a/city and we/at/her.

- Learn a few basic spelling rules, for example: 'I' before 'E' except after 'C', or when sounding like 'A' as in neighbour and weigh.

- Try to use cursive or joined up writing. This will help you to remember the 'feel' of the spelling in the same way that you remember your signature.

- Use a hand-held or computer spellchecker. Some of these will say the words for you.

- Set yourself the challenge of learning five new spellings each week. Make sure that you choose useful words that you need to know.

Handwriting and Presentation

It is important that pupils use cursive (joined up) writing as soon as possible for reasons of speed, fluency and support with spelling. This can be difficult for older students who have worked hard to raise their standard of printing to a reasonable level, as legibility will decline initially and they may lose heart. They should be persuaded that a cursive writing style is to their long-term advantage (Montgomery, 1997).

The completion of a handwriting questionnaire will enable students to analyse their own individual weaknesses and to focus on a specific area of their choosing for improvement.

Secondary pupils may find it hard to break entrenched habits, but if they assess their own handwriting, they are more likely to identify specific problems and be motivated to help themselves. Do not allow pupils to try and target several areas for improvement: instead encourage them to focus on one area at a time.

Although there are many commercial products for handwriting practice, it is cheaper to make individualised worksheets according to pupil age and need. A teacher or assistant could design handwriting, dot-to-dot, handwriting patterns, tracking and maze sheets in response to the specific problem areas identified by a pupil in their questionnaire, for example, the habit of omitting crosses on ascenders. Once prepared, sheets can be duplicated for the use of other pupils with similar problems.

Some pupils will have presentation problems because of underlying co-ordination difficulties. In such cases, handwriting practice alone will not help a pupil. It would be preferable to side-step the problem by using alternative strategies for the presentation and recording of work. This might include: the use of cloze sheets to ensure the pupil has a legible copy of essential information: word-processing; taped rather than written responses; support staff scribing for the pupil; the photocopying of maps and diagrams.

Lesson Plan

Learning objective
Pupils will target areas of their handwriting and presentation for improvement.

Resources required
- The Handwriting Questionnaire (see page 66).
- Plain, lined, carbon, tracing and handwriting paper.
- Pens, biros, pencils, gel pens, fine felt tips and pencil grips.
- Examples of old-fashioned handwriting practice sheets. These can be designed and photocopied for an individual or group as appropriate.

Activities
Pupils must first complete the handwriting questionnaire. Provide a range of resources: plain, lined, carbon, tracing and handwriting paper, a variety of pen grips, a variety of different styles of pens and handwriting practice sheets. Allow pupils to try some of the following activities. They could:

- Experiment with a variety of types and shapes of pens, pencils and pencil grips. There are several new types of pens on the market that have been designed to help with presentation, for example, pens and pencils designed specifically for left-handers. Just finding a pen to suit their writing style can instantly improve some pupils' presentation.

- Use two lines of narrow feint or shadowed paper as a guideline for letter height, with ascenders and descenders touching the second lines.

- Use carbon copy paper to show when they are applying too much pressure. Ask a pupil to try and write without leaving a second image. This is an effective way to show the degree of pressure they are exerting and why their hands and arms may ache.

- Scribble on scrap paper for 30 seconds before writing to relax their grip.

- Clench and stretch their fingers if their hands ache when writing, roll a piece of blu-tack between fingers and thumb or massage wrists and fingers to help muscles relax.

- Angle their paper if left-handed, tilting it in a clockwise direction at about a 20–30 degree angle to the right. When working in the classroom, left-handed pupils should always sit to the left of right-handed pupils.

- Realise the need for clean hands and for writing equipment to be in good working order.

- Use Dycem to hold rulers and mathematical equipment steady if accurate use of equipment presents problems. (Dycem is available from Boots.)

Pupils can complete handwriting practice sheets to get a feel for the flow of cursive writing. Provide a variety of 'home-made' sheets of writing patterns, letters and words for copying. Pupils can work in small groups so they can experiment with a collection of writing implements: biros, triangular-barrelled pencils, felt tips, pens and gel pens.

Handwriting Questionnaire

- Which arm would you throw a ball with?

- Which foot would you kick a ball with?

- Which hand do you use when cutting with scissors?

- Does your written work seem untidy when compared to work of friends of your age?

- Do teachers and friends say they cannot read your writing?

- Do you write very slowly?

- Are you aware of pressing very heavily or very lightly on the paper with your pen?

- Does your hand ache after you have completed writing on one side of a page?

- Do you have problems generally with presentation: copying maps, colouring within lines, drawing mathematical figures accurately, erasing neatly and copying diagrams of scientific apparatus?

- Look at some written work that you have completed recently. Do you join up or print letters when writing?

- Are the letters within words so squashed that it is difficult to distinguish one letter from another? Are the words cramped close together on the line?

- Is your writing very small or very large?

- Does your writing slope forwards or backwards to an extreme?

- Does your writing slope in different directions in one piece of work?

- Do you use capital letters in the middle of words?

- Does your writing always start at the margin on the left side of the page, or does it sometimes stray in from the edge?

- Does your writing 'sit on the line' or lie above and/or below the line?

- Do you always dot your 'i's and cross your 't's?

- Are there some letters that you don't know how to write?

- What area of your handwriting would you most like to improve?

Pupil Advice Sheet (Handwriting and Presentation)

- Make sure your hands and writing equipment are clean before you start work.

- Allow yourself enough space to work. Tidy away unnecessary clutter.

- Target one aspect of your handwriting for improvement at a time: making your writing larger, your words more appropriately spaced or crossing your 't's.

- Decide on one style of writing, and stick with it, preferably a simple style without loops or twirls.

- Decide on one angle or slope to your writing, and stick with it.

- Lean on something, a pad of paper or a mouse mat, to give a smoother surface.

- Use your non-writing hand to steady the paper.

- Some students find it useful to write with their paper supported on a file to give a sloping surface.

- Practise handwriting patterns to develop the flow of cursive writing.

- Some pupils find that pencil grips are useful to ensure they hold the pen correctly. Spongy grips can be comfortable if you have a tight grip.

- Experiment with different types of pens and pencils until you find one that makes your work look as neat as possible. Gel pens can be smooth, clean and give pleasing results.

- An elastic band wound around the barrel of a pen at a suitable height will keep your fingers up the pen and away from the nib.

- If your writing is very small, try using two lines of narrow-lined paper for each sentence to force you to enlarge your letters.

- If your hands ache because you press too heavily with your pen, try writing with carbon paper between two sheets of writing paper. Then practise writing so lightly that you don't leave a mark on the second sheet. Or try writing with a fine-tip felt pen, this will require less pressure to mark the paper.

- Scribble for 30 seconds on scrap paper to relax your hand before you start to write.

- If you are left-handed, always sit to the left of right-handed pupils when sharing a desk.

- Sit up straight with your back against the back of the chair and your feet on the floor.

- If you have glasses, wear them.

- Completing mazes, dot-to-dot and tracking exercises will help improve your pen control.

- Work on word-processing skills. A word-processed document will improve presentation instantly.

- Dycem can be fixed to the back of rulers and mathematical equipment to stop the instruments slipping during use.

Improving Co-ordination Skills Through Practical Activities

Many pupils have immature co-ordination skills. They may feel self-conscious practising these skills in front of their peers, but will be happy to carry out exercise programmes at home or during free time in school if these will improve their performance in PE and Games lessons.

Lessons could be described as circuit training if this made sessions more attractive to pupils.

Any refining of motor skills will improve a pupil's presentation.

Lesson Plan

A member of staff writes an individual 10 to 15–minute programme for a pupil using some exercises from the list below. The exercises should be completed on a regular basis during breaks, lunchtimes, free periods or at home. The pupil can keep a personal record of the exercises undertaken and the time or score achieved. The teacher monitors these records. Older pupils can work independently. Younger pupils may need some help with the recording. This is an area where peer support or pupil mentor systems are of use.

Learning objective
Pupils will improve their motor skills through co-ordination exercises.

Resources required
- Gym equipment: balls, skittles, mats, beanbags and hoops.

Activities
Gross motor skills

- Doing wall press-ups. Twenty press-ups against the wall.

- Sitting on a gym ball and rotating the body in a clockwise, then anticlockwise, direction.

- Crab walking for five metres forwards, backwards and sideways.

- Bouncing a ball with one hand. (If necessary, give pupils a beanbag to hold in the other hand to stop any mirroring of movement.)

- Playing skittles: use beanbags rather than balls to reduce chaos. How many skittles can be knocked down with three beanbags?

- Playing ball games: throwing and catching against a wall. First two hands, then left, then right hand only. How many throws can be completed successfully with each hand in two minutes?

- Kicking a ball between targets e.g. skittles. The distance between the two targets can be reduced as accuracy increases.

- Throwing beanbags into a container and into or through a hoop. How many beanbags hit the target?

- Looking straight ahead whilst throwing a beanbag from one hand to the other.

- Holding a ball in one hand, releasing one finger at a time to open out the palm totally, and then closing the hand around the ball in the same way.

- Walking along a line crossing feet on to the wrong side of the line. The pupil must keep looking ahead whilst walking.

- Walking heel to toe along a line, with a beanbag balanced on the head and hands kept down by the sides.

- Balancing on one foot at a time for 30 seconds. Repeating with eyes shut. As balance improves, change the surface from floor to carpet to mat to crash mat.

Resources required
- Coins.

- Empty plastic bottles.

- Stopwatches.

- Sheets of bubble wrap.

- Pegs and pegboard.

- Tweezers.

- Spent matches.

- Beads and bead laces.

- Dotted Maths paper.

Activities
Fine motor skills

- Turning over twelve 2p coins spread out on a flat surface with one hand and then the other. How many coins can be turned over with each hand in a minute?

- As with the first exercise, but picking up and posting the coins individually into a bottle held in the opposite hand. Recording the number of coins posted in 15 seconds with each hand.

- Working out how many bubbles in bubble wrap can be popped in a minute. Recording the number scored with each hand.

- Using flat-end tweezers to pick up spent matches and dropping them into a plastic bottle. How many matches can be put into the bottle in two minutes?

- Laying out playing cards on a table. Turning the cards over using left then right hand and timing this. How many cards can be turned over with each hand in 30 seconds?

- Working out how many accurate dots can be made on 'dotty' Maths paper in 30 seconds?

- Finding out how many beads can be threaded on a lace in one minute?

- Discovering how many pegs can be put in a pegboard in one minute?

- Holding several small objects (beads, buttons, paper clips) in one hand and then placing them individually on the table.

- Touching each finger on the right hand with the right thumb as quickly and accurately as possible. How many times can this be completed in 30 seconds?

7
Presentations

Oral Presentations

Many individuals are apprehensive about public speaking so it is important that presentation lessons are a positive experience. As pupils gain confidence and become experienced in oral presentations, feedback from their peers is useful. This could be from another pair, group or the whole class. All feedback must be positive and constructive.

If the group is very confident, videoing presentations will provide individuals with invaluable feedback. However, the member of staff present needs to be certain that this will be a positive experience for everyone.

Lesson Plan

Learning objective
Pupils will be able to make confident oral presentations.

Resources required
- A whiteboard or OHP.

Activities
A whole-class discussion about making oral presentations. Brainstorm positive and negative aspects of oral presentations. Discuss different ways of coping with any negative aspects.

A whole-class discussion about active listening and the importance of appropriate behaviour when other pupils are speaking. The class divides into pairs. One partner talks about their favourite book, film or television programme while their partner feigns boredom and disinterest by yawning, appearing distracted and failing to take any interest in what is being said. The roles are then exchanged so that both partners experience the discomfort of talking to someone who is not listening.

Divide the class into pairs. Each pair is to plan a talk to be delivered to three other pairs on a topic of their choice. The talk should last for three to five minutes. They should discuss the following points with their partners:

- Will the information be at a basic or advanced level? How much does the audience already know about the topic? Will the audience understand topic specific vocabulary?

- What information should be left in and what should be taken out? Is it better to concentrate on a few main points rather than risk confusing the audience by giving too much detail?

- How many sections should the talk be divided into?

- Are visual aids necessary? What will they be? Will IT be necessary? How does the IT equipment work?

- How should the talk be organised? Will one person be responsible for the visual aids as the other person talks? Will they speak alternately?

- How much input is needed from the audience? Will questions be taken during your presentation or at the end?

Each pair then prepares their talk for the following week/lesson.

Distribute the Pupil Advice Sheet (Giving a Presentation).

Pupil Advice Sheet (Giving a Presentation)

- Prepare thoroughly. The more you prepare, the more confident you will be.

- When organising notes for a talk, divide them into sections. Write down the title of each section clearly on a postcard and underline it. Against each title note down a few key words to act as a memory prompt for the order of your points.

- Make your notes very clear. Number the cards or papers. Thread them together in order with a lace through a hole punched in the top left-hand corner. These precautions will make it easier to find your place if you get lost.

- Talk your presentation through aloud as many times as possible. The more familiar it is, the more confident you will feel. If you start with full notes, and every time you run through the talk reduce the notes, you are more likely to recall the details from memory and be able to speak naturally.

- If you practise your talk aloud, you will be able to keep speaking even if you lose your train of thought. Eventually you will be able to repeat your talk like the words of a familiar song.

- Time your talk and cut out sections or add information to make sure it is the right length.

- Begin with a brief introduction: list the main areas that you will be covering. At the end of your talk, review the key issues briefly.

- Speak clearly and slowly. Look up at your audience to help your voice carry. If looking at the group makes you nervous, look beyond them towards the back of the room.

- Posters and acetates are useful as visual aids and will give you a few moments to check on your next point. Remember to position your visual aids so that the audience can see them clearly.

- Support your points with examples and statistics to add weight to your argument.

- Stick to the talk you have planned. Try not to go off at a tangent.

- Decide whether you want the audience to ask questions during the talk or afterwards. Questions during a talk can interrupt your flow and may be boring if the question is of specific interest to just one person, but audience participation can make a talk more entertaining.

- Check your appearance before the talk so that you can't worry about it during your presentation.

Group Work

The ability to be able to function effectively as the member of a team is important for a variety of reasons.

- Group work can be a valuable source of support and reassurance when topics are unfamiliar.

- Some individuals learn best through oral input and discussion.

- Open discussion gives opportunities to develop balanced opinions.

- Good communication is an essential skill for life.

- Employers value their employees' ability to work with others and pupils need to practise the art of negotiation and compromise.

Lesson Plan

Learning objective
To enable pupils to participate effectively in group discussion.

Resources required
- A whiteboard or OHP.

Activities
Pupils are divided into small groups this may require some discrete structuring by the teacher to ensure a good balance of personalities.

Each group thinks of and records some of the advantages of group work, for example:

- Everyone has had different experiences, and so a group will think of more ideas than one person will.

- There is more choice over tasks to be completed. Individuals can use their strengths and focus on the aspect of the topic they enjoy most.

- Working in a group helps to maintain concentration.

- Questions asked within the group can be worked out together.

The teacher delegates roles within the group: chairperson, scribe, observer and reporter. All members will be asked questions after the presentation.

The chairperson will be responsible for reading out the instructions, getting the discussion started, making sure everyone has a chance to speak and that this is orderly, keeping the group focussed and summarising final conclusions.

The scribe or secretary will record key points objectively, note any differing viewpoints and check that the whole group agrees with the concluding summary.

The observer will monitor individual input and collect information. Did any one person ramble, monopolise the discussion, interrupt too often or did everyone contribute in a positive way and listen carefully to the opinions of others?

The reporter will be responsible for reporting the views of the group to the rest of the class in an unbiased way.

Each group chooses or is given a topic for discussion: from a list on the whiteboard or OHP. These might include such topics as:

- School uniform is an infringement of human rights.
- Cars should be banned from cities.
- Vivisection is a necessary evil.
- Television censorship should be stricter.
- No one under 21 should hold a driving licence.

The group discusses their topic: for 15 minutes, collects arguments for and against the motion and puts together some shared conclusions.

The reporter feeds back the group's conclusions to the class. The class asks questions of different members of the group.

The teacher gives feedback: did each group listen to the other groups; did each group keep to their time constraints; did the members of the group keep to their allotted tasks? The class gives positive comments on other students' performances.

Pupil Advice Sheet (Group Discussions)

- If you are confident and articulate in group situations, try not to dominate the discussion, but use your skills to include the quieter members of the group.

- If you know you are not a confident contributor in a group, try to speak at least once during the first session, twice in the second session and so on. You do not have to speak for long, just make brief points.

- Talk to the other group members outside the session so that you feel at ease in their company.

- If you find it hard to be a good speaker, be a good listener. If you listen carefully, any points that you do make will be valid and useful.

- During group sessions, sit between friendly, supportive individuals.

- Try to act as if you are confident, even if you don't feel it.

- When making your points, speak to everyone in the group, not just particular individuals.

- If someone else is speaking, jot down a key word to remind you of the point you want to make when they have finished, then listen to what they are saying.

- Be brief. Make your point without waffling. Waffling will confuse your audience.

- Respond positively to the contributions of others, even if you do not always agree with them. Ask questions to show interest in their opinions.

- Remember that the discussion is not to show how much you already know, but to help you learn.

- Afford others the respect you would like them to give you.

8
Revision and Exam Techniques

How to Revise

Everyone's approach to revision will differ. There is no right or wrong way to revise, only what works for the individual.

Throughout any revision period a good state of health is very important: pupils need plenty of exercise, to eat healthily, have adequate amounts of sleep and maintain a positive attitude.

To be successful revision must be active. A pupil must think about information in order to remember it.

It makes sense to revise using as many senses as possible:

- If pupils are visual learners encourage the use of mind maps, posters, ICT, highlighter pens, illustrations and videos.

- Auditory learners should use tapes, reading or reciting aloud, rhymes, group revision and discussion.

- Kinaesthetic learners should use role-play, games, writing and re-writing and revising in short bursts.

(See Chapter 2.)

Lesson Plan

Learning objective
Pupils develop an understanding of the range of revision methods available to them.

Resources required
- File cards.

- Class text.

- Coloured pencils.

- Commercial revision materials: books, videos, tapes and CDs.

Activities

- The teacher distributes the Pupil Advice Sheet (revision methods) and runs through some of these (see pages 80–2). Pupils work in pairs or small groups to discuss any techniques they currently use and feedback to the class. Each group suggests one technique that they have discussed, and explains the strengths and possible weaknesses of that particular approach.

"We feel that we learn well from group discussion. Some of the advantages of this revision method would be: other people may have understood better than you, their notes may be easier to understand or they are able to explain a specific subject really clearly. They are happy to spend time going over information they have revised because it helps them to remember, and we are happy to listen because it helps our understanding. You can ask friends questions there aren't time for in class, and working things out together is reassuring because you don't feel stupid. Disadvantages would be that it is easy to be distracted if you start talking about other things, your friends might prefer to work at a different time and might not want to revise the same topics, their notes might be different to yours so that you get confused, and some people don't do their share, they just let you do all of the work."

- Each pupil makes revision notes on a file card from an appropriate page or chapter of a class textbook: selecting and recording key words on the card using colour, highlighters, different writing styles and abbreviations.

  Supplementary details, facts or dates can be added using numbering, mnemonics or illustrations.

  Each pupil makes a mind map of a topic from these revision cards following the instructions under 'Mind Mapping' in Chapter 6 (see page 51).

- Review some of the commercially produced materials, e.g. watch an exam board or BBC video; listen to an MFL tape; look at a CD ROM or compare different types of revision books. Some of these revision texts specialise in a certain type of format: pictorially displayed information, pre-printed question-and-answer cards, old question papers or an overview of the basics. Different pupils will prefer different approaches.

- Pupils revising for end-of-topic tests could design advice posters or revision booklets as part of their revision for pupils who will be covering the module next year. This will give relevance to their work and encourage them to pick out the main facts and to be clear and succinct. The advice of pupils who have recently taken an exam often seems more credible to younger pupils.

- Stress the care that must be taken when reading test papers. Give the pupils written instructions in the form of the test below.

Speed Test

You have exactly two minutes to complete this test, so work quickly.

- Read all of the questions before you start the test.

- Write your name and age in the top left-hand corner.

- Write your date of birth under your name.

- Write today's date in the top right-hand corner.

- List the number of exam subjects you hope to take.

- Describe in two sentences what you hope to do when you leave school.

- Have you researched this career at all?

- Who would you go to for information about this? Delete as necessary: librarian, teacher, parents, friends.

- List three of your aspirations for the future.

- Complete the first question only.

Pupil Advice Sheet (Revision Methods)

We all learn in different ways. You may not use the same methods as your friends, your teacher or members of your family: work in the way you prefer. All revision methods work best when they are *active*; that is when your brain has to engage with and think about the information.

Little and often

- Most individuals are able to concentrate for 30-40 minutes before their attention wavers.

- There is no point trying to revise when you are not focused, so build regular breaks and variety into revision sessions. Frequent short periods of revision will be more effective than hours of cramming.

- If you really get stuck on something, leave it and come back to it later. Your brain will make links and solve the problem while you do something else.

- Energetic activities provide the best breaks if you are revising for long periods: take the dog for a walk, go for a bike ride, run round the block or walk up and down the stairs 20 times. Your brain will be refreshed by the increased supply of oxygen resulting from physical activity.

Organisation

- Revision will be much easier if your files are up to date and well ordered. Hole punch handouts and separate essays and notes for different modules with coloured dividers. Have several files and folders rather than one that is overflowing.

- Condense all the information from one module onto a side of A4 with diagrams and cartoons. Use coloured pens and highlighters to make this overview of the information as visually appealing as possible.

- Work out a realistic revision timetable and stick to it, setting yourself targets that you know you will be able to achieve. Build in flexible time to use if you have a headache or are invited to a good party unexpectedly. Leave the few days before your exams free to go over gaps in your understanding.

- Decide when you work most effectively and learn new or difficult material then.

- Mix sessions revising easy topics with sessions spent revising those topics that you find harder.

- Keep your workplace stocked with spare equipment: pens, paper, rulers, rubbers and highlighters. Make sure that the area is at a comfortable temperature, properly ventilated and well lit.

Senses

- You are more likely to remember if you use all of your senses.

- Visual – make notes with coloured pens on coloured paper, use highlighters, and convert your notes into cartoons, time lines, flow charts and diagrams.

- Auditory – revise with friends or family. Ask your friends to test you, discuss topics with your family members, pets, anyone who will listen. Read your notes aloud. Explain what you have learnt to yourself. Record yourself reading information on tape and listen to this in the car, on the bus, in the bath or whilst walking to school.

- Kinaesthetic – write out key words or scribble your notes out over and over again. Walk around the room as you revise, reading aloud in time with your steps. Write out key points on Post-it notes, assemble them on your wall and move them around to get an idea of how the information is related.

File cards

- A popular way to revise is to condense notes into summaries written on file cards. Use different coloured cards for different topics.

- Cards are a way of easily chunking revision sessions: you could read five cards aloud before your evening meal, or four cards in the bath, or make a mind map from one card before you go to bed. Cards will expand or contract to fill the time available.

- Just making the cards will make you think about the information.

- Cards are quick visual reminders of key points; keep copies of those cards you find hardest to remember in your pocket and read them during the day.

- Use numbers, different writing styles, drawings, lists, different coloured pens and highlighters to make the cards visually attractive.

- Ask a friend to test you on the cards; read them aloud; turn them over and rewrite or recite the information from memory; make new cards from old ones; tape yourself reading the cards and then listen to the tape as you look at them again. The potential for adaptation to personal taste is endless.

Remember – the cards are there for you to revise from. Do not spend all of your time making the cards and then leave no time for revision.

Mnemonics

- Mnemonics are memory triggers: funny or rude sentences, poems or clue words. For example, to remember the planets in their order moving away from the sun, take the first letter of each word from this sentence, '**M**y **v**ery **e**ducated **m**other **j**ust **s**erved **u**s **n**ine **p**izzas' and you have Mercury, Venus, Earth, Mars, Jupiter, Saturn, Uranus, Neptune, Pluto. The more individual and personal the mnemonic, the more memorable it will be.

Understanding

- The more you understand, the less you have to learn by rote, so it makes sense to understand as much as you can. If you have not understood a topic, ask your teacher to explain it in a different way.

- Attend any revision classes and workshops that are offered to you. Try to build up a positive relationship with your teachers. If they see you making an effort, they will be more likely to help you.

- Other pupils may understand your confusions more than teaching staff, so ask peers for explanations. They may be able to explain a difficult topic in everyday, as opposed to specialist, language.

- Read easier textbooks. Use Key Stage 3 books to support GCSE level work. They will help to make basic information clear.

Mind maps

- Summarise all the information from a module into one mind map and blu-tack the mind maps to the wall or ceiling of your bedroom. Study the mind maps before you go to sleep and you will remember the overall pattern of the notes and the key words within that pattern.

- If you create a mind map for each end-of-module test throughout the year, you will have a good collection to use for exams.

- The mere act of translating information into diagram form will force you to think about how the facts relate to each other.

Old papers

- Working through old exam papers is a useful activity for practising exam technique and getting a feel for time allowances.

- Alternatively answers to papers could be completed in note or mind map form.

Group revision

- Pair or group revision can be very effective if you are an auditory learner.
- Take it in turns to teach topics to each other. If you restrict the amount of time that each person is allowed, they will be forced to identify the main points and issues: 'Tell us everything you know about photosynthesis in two minutes'.
- When working with others, devise a timetable and stick to it: 30 minutes discussion on one topic, have a break, test each other on vocabulary for 20 minutes, and then make a mind map on the first topic.
- If your friends are more interested in current gossip, they will be a distraction. You must be disciplined.
- You can revise with others while you go for a walk or bike ride. You do not have to sit indoors.

Rote learning

- Rote learning is learning facts in parrot fashion. This is useful in the short term, to cram information immediately before a test, but not if you need to retain the information for any length of time.

Pupil Advice Sheet (Exam Techniques)

- Arrive at the exam in plenty of time with the correct (and spare) equipment.

- If your mind goes completely blank when you turn the question paper over, start jotting down a few general points to get into gear.

- Sometimes it is useful to write down mnemonics as soon as the exam starts to free up your short-term memory.

- Read the paper carefully. It is very easy to misread one word and alter the whole meaning of a question.

- Check instructions. How many questions must you answer and from what sections?

- Look to see if the questions have a mark value and spend an appropriate amount of time on each. There is no point in spending 30 minutes on a question that is only worth two marks.

- Plan your use of time. Put your watch on the table in front of you where it is clearly visible. Do not be tempted to write for longer than the amount of time you have allotted for that specific question.

- Decide which questions look possible and which are to be avoided. Start with the easiest one to give you confidence.

- If your mind goes blank, jot down a few points and key words to stimulate your memory and get you started. If you get stuck don't waste time, start another question; the answer will come to you as you work.

- Draw out a rough plan or mind map of your answer before you start to write.

- Underline any key words in questions: 'describe', 'contrast', 'compare'. These words will describe exactly what you are being asked to do and how to do it.

- Concentrate on answering the question that has been set, not the one that you would have liked to answer. Check back occasionally to ensure that you are doing this. Select relevant information. Do not simply write down everything that you know.

- Keep your work as neat as possible. It will be less irritating for the examiner and easier to mark.

- Use diagrams if appropriate, they may explain more clearly than words.

- Try to allow time for proof reading, but if you do run short of time jot down your final points in note form.

- Do not waste time worrying about how much anyone else is writing or what you wish you had revised. Pay attention to what you can do now.

Pupil Advice Sheet (Dealing with Exam Anxiety)

- Think about things that you can do something about, rather than those you can't. Don't just worry about things, do something about them: listen to that tape on the way home, learn that French vocabulary while you're in the bath. Every little bit of work that you are able to do will help.

- Think positively. Tick off all of the topics you have revised.

- Focus on specific tasks rather than wider issues. Practise an old Maths exam paper rather than speculate on what might happen if you fail the Maths exam.

- Think about the present. Do not think about the exam you did in the morning; concentrate on what you are doing now.

- Even if you feel that you have left revision too late, focus on what you have done rather than what you haven't. You have been studying these subjects for several years on a regular basis and are certain to remember some of the content.

- Feel able to use common sense and general knowledge to support answers.

- Keep fit and healthy. Get enough sleep and exercise. While you sleep, your brain will sort and order information to help you to make sense of it. Exercise will boost your brainpower by getting more oxygen to the brain. Eat sensibly; always make sure you have a good breakfast on the morning of an exam. Toast or cereal releases energy slowly over a long period and will keep you alert. Drink plenty of water to ward off headaches.

- Build relaxation time into your schedule, so that you can go out and enjoy yourself without feeling guilty.

- Plan treats for the end of the exams.

- Reassure yourself that you have prepared as best you can. Ultimately you can only do your best. Exams only measure certain abilities and there are many other aspects of your personality: humour, motivation, determination, empathy, creativity, perception, courage, perseverance, kindness, social skills, energy and tolerance that will relate more closely to success and happiness in life.

- Even if you fail an exam, you can always re-sit. In a year's time none of your friends or family will remember your grades. Future contacts need never know.

Appendices and Glossary

Howard Gardner's Multiple Intelligences

- **Kinaesthetic**   A wide range of practical aptitudes, dance, drama and creative skills. This intelligence will cover physical and sporting ability.

- **Musical**   Skill in composing and playing music and an appreciation of rhythm.

- **Visual-spatial**   Artistic talent and visualisation skills. This intelligence is linked closely to practical creativity.

- **Logical/mathematical**   Ability with numbers and scientific thought. An individual with talent in this area will enjoy problem solving, precision, abstract thought and logic.

- **Interpersonal**   The ability to empathise and work with others. Individuals with this intelligence will be popular and enjoy social interaction.

- **Linguistic**   A skill in all forms of written and oral literacy: a general ability with language. Anyone with this intelligence will be gifted in reading, writing, listening and discussion.

- **Intrapersonal**   Good self-knowledge and understanding. Individuals with this form of intelligence will know how to motivate themselves and make the best of their abilities.

Multiple Intelligences

What multiple intelligences do you feel you have and why?

What multiple intelligences does your partner feel you have and why?

My multiple intelligences	My partner's multiple intelligences

Reminder

1 Kinaesthetic intelligence = practical skill, good at sport.

2 Linguistic intelligence = good with words and language.

3 Visual spatial intelligence = artistic and creative.

4 Interpersonal intelligence = able to get on with and understand other people.

5 Mathematical logical intelligence = ability with numbers and problem solving.

6 Intrapersonal intelligence = knowing how **you** work and think.

7 Musical intelligence = able to appreciate and make music.

Reading Techniques

SKIM = to get the main idea of a passage

SCAN = to look for a specific piece of information

CLOSE READING = to read a passage word for word

Would you skim, scan or read closely in the following situations?

1   Looking up a phone number in the telephone directory.

2   Reading an essay title.

3   Reading a long, boring letter from your aunt.

4   To see what time your bus went.

5   Looking at a library book to see if you could use it for your project.

6   To see how much flour you needed for a recipe.

Now think of two more examples for each reading technique.

```
SKIM
1.

2.



```

```
SCAN
1.

2.



```

```
READ CAREFULLY
1.

2.



```

Increasing Silent Reading Speed

Choose a book that you can read quite easily. Read silently for a minute.

Count how many words you have read and write this number down.

DATE	NUMBER OF WORDS READ
• Day 1	....
• Day 2	....
• Day 3	....
• Day 4	....
• Day 5	....
• Day 6	....
• Day 7	....

- Read another passage for a minute from the same book the following evening and record your reading rate again. Concentrate on reading as quickly as you can, but still try to absorb the meaning of the text. Do this every evening for two weeks and you will find that your reading speed will gradually increase.

- Try to take in three or four words at a time rather than every word.

- Do not allow yourself to backtrack to check on words, but keep your eyes moving forwards. Your brain will fill in the gaps.

- Put a ruler or index card under the line that you are reading and move it steadily down the page to maintain pace. Alternatively, use your finger or pen as a pointer and move it along the line of print.

Using Context to Guess a Word

- Guess the meaning of the nonsense word in the passage. Each nonsense word could be replaced by several different words so there is no one right answer.

Thomas's oyhiuh sent him some frcty for his birthday. On Saturday Thomas ytre into town with his nhux. They went into the apyu shop and bought Nibbbles. Nibbles mbgf a mouse. He had white cdeq and uybf eyes. They needed somewhere fpoil Nibbles to live, so they bought him a pvwmi. The pvwmi had a little house for Nibbles to mucez in zxyl an exercise byjo.

- Check your answers with your partner.

- Now try this passage.

Barry the giant lived on gynf edge of the town in a huge kdbe. Barry was a friendly giant who ydsge the people in the town in ongvd ways. He mended dsaks that had ujve down and replaced missing ogbsd tiles and inhg pots after heavy winds. After a particularly retbv winter unfcd, Barry rebuilt the town unsl so that the people could jkung the river.

- See if you can write a passage with some nonsense words for your partner to correct.

Dictionary Work

All of these words begin with the letter 'D'. Do you know how to or can you use a dictionary to find out what they are?

d – – – – – – – – (9 letters)   A canine disease. Paint for use on walls.

d – – – – – – (7 letters)   Great pleasure.

d – – – (4 letters)   The floor or storey of a ship or bus.

d – – – (4 letters)   A valley.

d – – – (4 letters)   A shallow bowl.

d – – – – – – – – (9 letters)   To take to pieces.

Look up the definitions of six words in the dictionary beginning with the letter 'S'. Write the words down on the back of this paper.

Write down a short definition of each word and the number of letters in the word in the spaces below.

Ask your partner to identify each word.

Word   Meaning

s.........................(   )..

s.........................(   )..

s.........................(   )..

s........................ (   )..

s........................ (   )..

s.........................(   )..

Make up a Sentence that Uses Each Word

You may need to use a dictionary.

Example:

cram indolent priest =

The indolent priest will cram himself in the car.

1   permit shoulder drool

2   irrelevant recycle robot

3   diction pastime spaniel

4   coriander maid infuriate

5   guffaw adolescent chrome

6   bluff sergeant ferocious

Now choose words for your partner to put into a sentence.

* ....

* ....

* ....

* ....

Boring Words

Replace the boring words with ones that are more interesting.

Walk/walked

Uncle Ted and Auntie Kat <u>walked</u> down the road towards the station. They were <u>walking</u> slowly as they looked at the train timetable. They were nearly run over by a lorry when they crossed the road and had to <u>walk</u> quickly to the other side. 'We better hurry, the train goes in five minutes' said Ted. They began to <u>walk</u> quickly.

'Don't <u>walk</u> like that', said Kat.

'I'm trying to <u>walk</u> quickly said Ted. 'You <u>walk</u> slowly if you like, but I am going to <u>walk</u> quickly'.

More interesting words that you could use: run dawdle hurry stroll race sprint amble saunter stride march trot rush plod wander.

Write a passage for your partner. The passage must use the word 'nice' at least five times. Your partner has to change each 'nice' for a more interesting word that will make sense in the passage.

Write another short passage each. You and your partner can choose from 'get', 'good', 'bad', 'big' or 'said' as your boring word.

Compound Words

Compound words are made when two words are put together. For example:

Net + ball = netball. Bird + cage = birdcage. Egg + cup = eggcup.

You have two minutes to think of as many compound words as you can.

1 haircut	
2	

How many new compound words can you create?

Give their meaning.

WORD	MEANING
1 Handsock	A mitten

94

Memory Grid 1

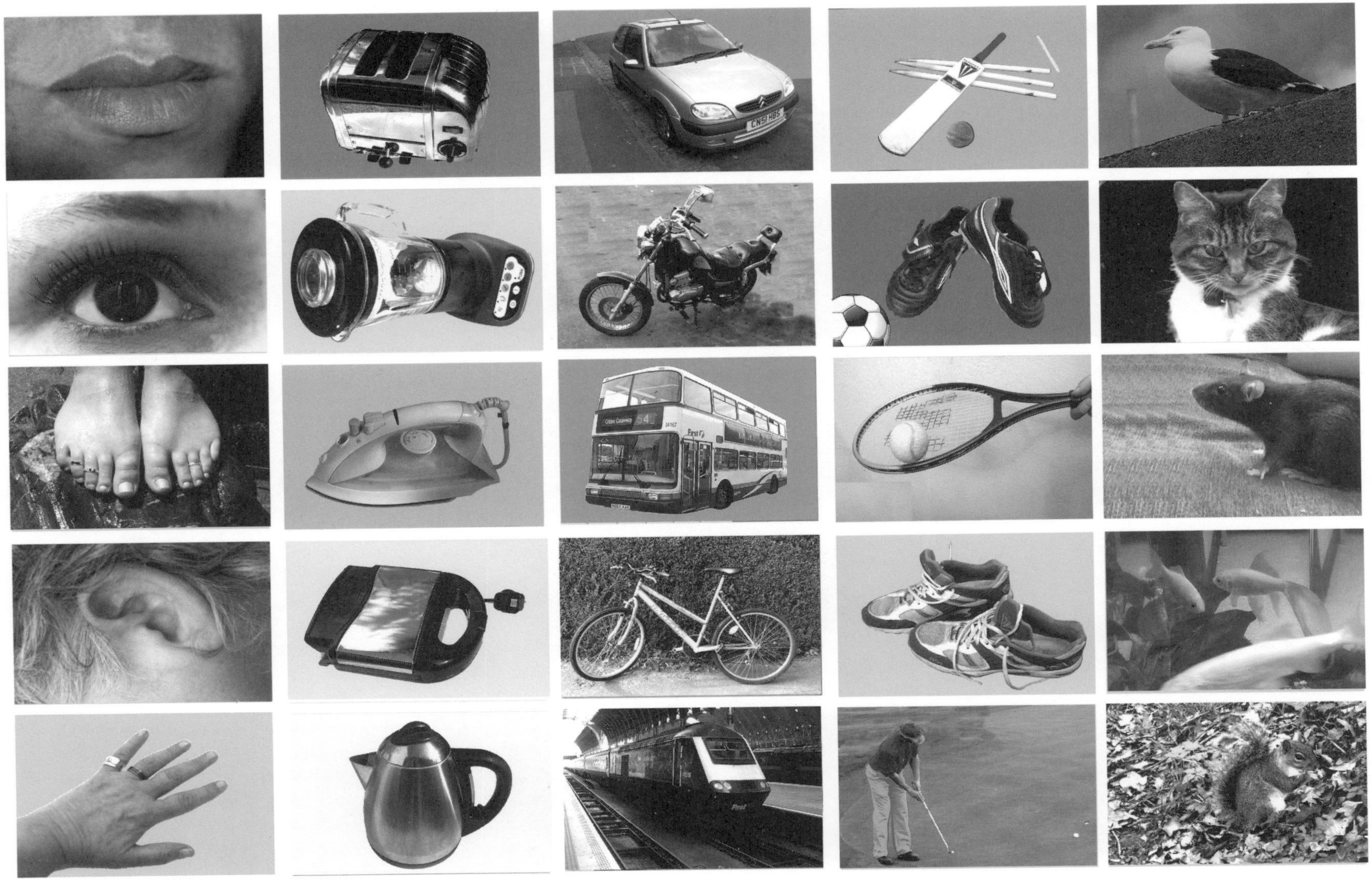

Memory Grid 2

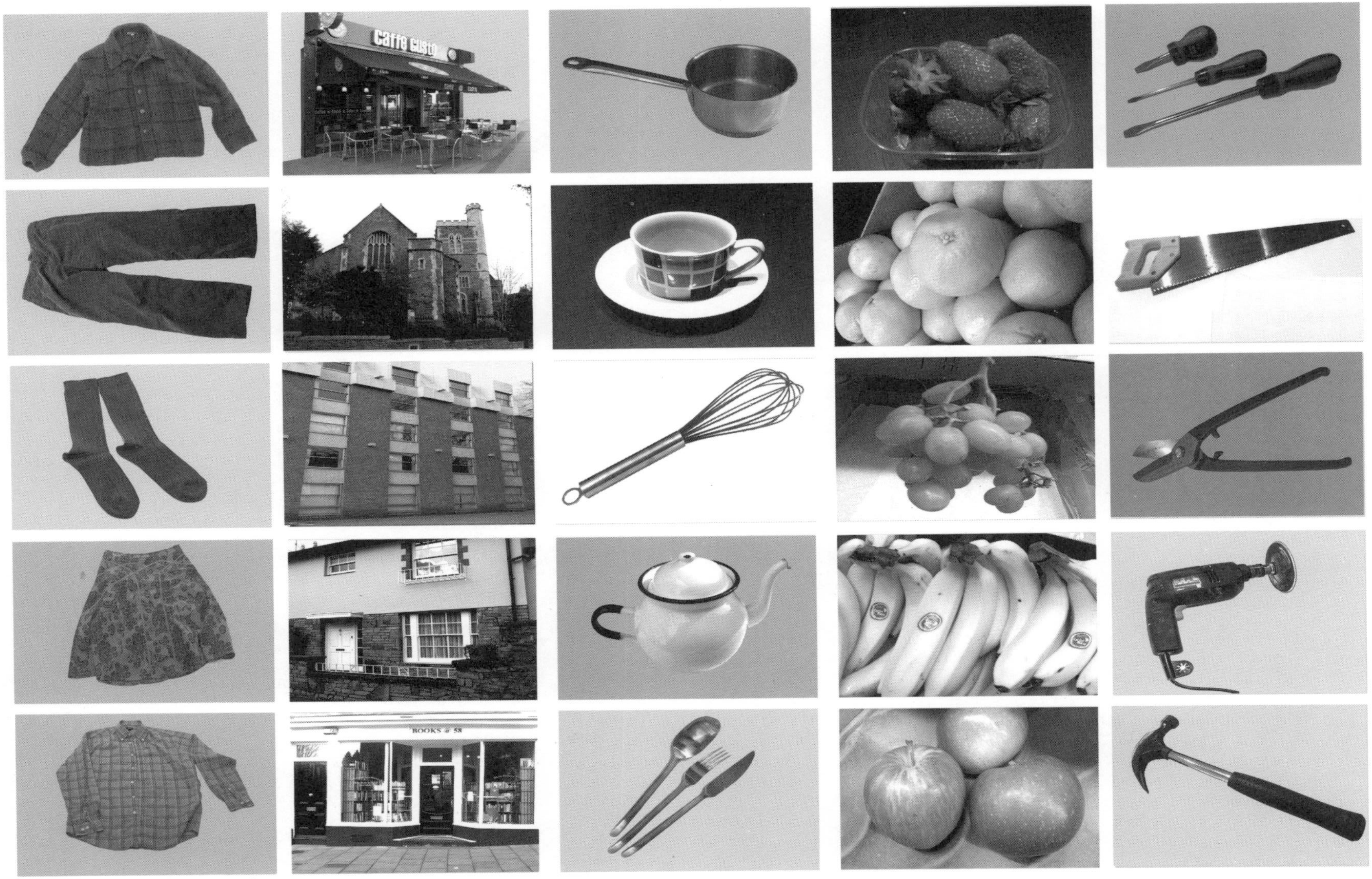

99

Synonyms

Words with a similar meaning to each other are called synonyms. Big, enormous, huge, massive and gigantic are all synonyms.

Find the odd one out

Underline the word in each line that is not a synonym:

1   disgusting   offensive   nasty   unpleasant   kind

2   rotate   spin   twirl   finish   revolve   circle

3   accident   head   disaster   mishap   calamity   misfortune

4   fence   barrier   wall   barricade   fibre   railing

Look in the thesaurus for some words that have the same meaning and write them out below. Put in one word that has a different meaning. See if your partner can find the odd one out.

1   ....

2   ....

3   ....

4   ....

5   ....

Homophones

Words that sound the same, but are spelt differently are called homophones. An example of a homophone would be: beech (a type of tree) and beach (the sandy sea shore).

Put each of the words below into a sentence to show their meaning and then draw an illustration to help you to remember the difference.

Example: sale and sail.

The church jumble sale was held in the village hall.

The boat had a large white sail.

1   whole and hole.

2   route and root.

3   saw and sore.

Think of some more mnemonics that would help you to remember confusing words.

Hot and Cold

Put these words into an order. Explain the order you have chosen to your partner.

Example: mild   cold   freezing   chilly   warm   sweltering   hot.

New order = freezing, cold, chilly, mild, warm, hot, sweltering.

These words have been ordered according to temperature.

1   small   enormous   massive   tiny   average   large

   _____   _____   _____   ____   _____   ____

- -

2   apple   cherry   grape   melon   grapefruit   tangerine

   _____   _____   _____   _____   _____   _____

- -

3   red   orange   yellow   green   blue   indigo   violet

   _____   _____   _____   _____   _____   _____   _____

- -

4   forty-one   nineteen   fifty-six   seven   sixty-five

   _____   _____   _____   _____   _____

- -

5   netball   hockey   basketball   rugby   tennis

   _____   _____   _____   _____   _____

- -

6   terrace   hovel   semi-detached   cottage   palace   mansion

   _____   _____   _____   _____   _____   _____

- -

7   biscuit   balloon   banana   beer   bicycle   bamboo

   _____   _____   _____   _____   _____   _____

- -

8   Peru   Scotland   France   Switzerland   China   USA

   _____   _____   _____   _____   _____   _____

- -

See if you can make up five lists of words for your partner to order.

Your partner must say why they chose that order. It might be different to yours.

Self-Assessment Questionnaire

What are my learning style and intelligence preferences?

....104..

....

....

What are my learning strengths?

For example: I am a fast reader, I discuss well in class, I understand best when I do something practical, I enjoy working by myself.

....

....

....

How can I use these strengths to help myself in school?

....

....

....

What are my weaker areas?

For example: I do not always understand what I am being asked to write about in essays, my spelling isn't very good, I find it hard to remember French vocabulary, I am a slow reader.

....

....

....

What strategies can I use to help myself overcome these difficulties?

....

....

....

What do I need to target immediately?

For example: organise my files, develop cursive handwriting, participate more in class, get more sleep.

....

....

....

What will I need to think about in the future?

For example: learning to touch type, attending subject revision sessions, GCSE or A Level choices, increasing my reading speed.

....
....
....

Glossary

auditory learner   a person who learns best by listening and discussing.

cursive handwriting   joined up handwriting.

expressive vocabulary   the words that you use.

gross motor control   a person's ability to control large physical movement in activities like running, jumping and playing sport.

kinaesthetic learner   an individual who learns best through doing.

learning style   how a student or pupil learns.

linear notes   notes that follow a logical sequence across or down the page.

metacognition   learning how to learn.

mind map   notes made in a visual patterned form on one piece of paper.

mnemonics   memory aids. 'Richard of York gave battle in vain' to remember the order of the colours of the rainbow: red, orange, yellow, green, blue, indigo and violet.

multiple intelligences   Howard Gardner's theory that there are several ways in which individuals can show ability.

oral   the spoken word, information given through speech.

proof reading   to check work for errors.

receptive vocabulary   the words that you can understand.

scan   to look for specific information in written material, for example, the time of a train or a phone number in a directory.

skim   to read to get the general idea of something, for example, a book about rabbits to see if it was suitable for a five year old.

subject specific vocabulary   subject words, for example, in Science: ions, temperature, thermometer, solution, chlorine, conductor.

visual aids   something that you can look at to help you understand: a picture, a video, a diagram or a poster.

visual learner   someone who learns best by using their eyes.

visualisation   imagining a sequence of events or pictures in your mind.

Bibliography

Buzan, T. (2003) *Mind Maps for Kids*. London: Thorsons.

Cook, V. (2004) *Accomodating Brocolli in the Cemetary*. London: Profile.

Edwards, J. (1998) *Look! Listen! Think!* Warwickshire: Prim-Ed.

Gardner, H. (1993) *Frames of Mind: The Theory of Multiple Intelligences*. New York: Basic.

McLean, B. and Wood, R. (2004) *Target Reading Comprehension*. Edinburgh: Barrington Stoke.

Montgomery, D. (1997) *Spelling*. London: Cassell.

Quinion, M. (2004) *POSH and other Language Myths*. London: Penguin.

Rickerby, S. and Lambert, S. (1994a) *Listening Skills KS1*. Birmingham: Questions.

Rickerby, S. and Lambert, S. (1994b) *Listening Skills KS2*. Birmingham: Questions.

Wray, D. and Lewis, M. (2000) *Literacy in the Secondary School*. London: Fulton.